BALLET CHANGED M

Ballet Hoo! The Story of the Cha

ROD MORGAN with ANDREW SPARKE

APS PUBLICATIONS

Cover photograph courtesy Phil Ryley

ISBN 9781912309580

APS Publications,
4 Oakleigh Road,
Stourbridge,
West Midlands,
DY8 2JX

www.andrewsparke.com

For Keith Horsfall and all the flourishing graduates from this and every other Leaps and Bounds programme. Thanks Keith for coming on the ride with me.

Andrew Sparke

foreword

by Sir Christopher Frayling, Chair of Arts Council England

TOO MUCH TO ASK?

The story of Leaps & Bounds

When I became Chair of the Arts Council in 2004, one of my priorities was to explore the connections between the arts and the behaviour of young people - especially disaffected young people.

I had known Rod Morgan for many years (we taught together at the University of Bath in the 1970s and we still both live in the same city) and shared his views on the demonisation of teenagers, and on more creative solutions than locking people up all the time. I was very keen to explore these ideas in an arts context.

So I was delighted in February 2007 to be taking part in a seminar at the RIBA in London to reflect on some of the findings of the highly successful Leaps and Bounds Project – featured in the Channel 4 series Ballet Changed My Life: Ballet Hoo! The audience was varied, including representatives from

education and dance, Whitehall and local authorities – and even the Lord Chief Justice.

Youth At Risk's charismatic Chief Executive Neil Wragg had also invited some of the young people who had taken part to speak about the effect that the series and the project had had on them

personally. In the event, their contributions proved to be moving, eloquent and inspirational. This was important because so often with arts and media projects, after transmission the participants are left high and dry when the cameras have moved on.

The message, which came over loud and clear, was that this had been a groundbreaking experiment which combined ballet and 'personal development training' to stunning effect on the participants and project partners, and resulted in an excellent live dance performance at the Birmingham Hippodrome, justly identified by Deborah Crane in the Sunday Times as one of the three dance highlights of 2006. It had also turned into one of the top arts television programmes of recent years with great reviews.

'The kind of truly inspirational story that most TV producers would sell their kids to make.' (The Guardian, September 2006)

'This is one of those rare occasions when television acts as a genuine force for good.' (The Times, 20 September 2006)

'The project is all about overturning preconceptions … a testament to the transformative power of art.' (The Independent, 10 September 2006)

'Their Romeo and Juliet is a triumph! … Once they stumbled but now they soar … It is amazing how completely these unlikely dancers fill their roles. Shireenah is every inch a queen … the curtain call could make a programme in itself.' (The Observer, 1 October 2006)

'A series that's shaping up to be a life-affirming treasure.' (Radio Times, 23–29 September 2006)

I was particularly pleased and proud that the Arts Council had invested £100k in the initiative, developing our partnership with Channel 4 and Diverse Productions, backing an innovative idea

and helping it to happen on a grand scale, and bringing the work of one of our regularly funded organisations Birmingham Royal Ballet to a nation-wide audience. The series challenged perceptions both of 'young people at risk' and of 'high art' and it put over the fact that 'excellence' and 'access' are not in any way antithetical – rather, they reinforce one another. This can't be said often enough.

When we were approached by Roy Ackerman of Diverse Productions in 2005, we did think more than twice about our getting involved. The project was perceived to be highly risky, not least in the unconventional methods of the lead organisation Youth At Risk, which had not been applied to the arts before; plus there was the range of complex partnerships across different services and disciplines in Birmingham and the West Midlands.

The Arts Council had already begun to put a greater focus on work with young people at risk, looking for imaginative 'beacon' projects to explore this territory further and bring it to wider public attention. We committed to the project when it became clear that it involved a highly imaginative new way of engaging young people in dance education and performance work. The project also aimed to leave an important legacy. I should add that there's a lot of valuable arts and social inclusion work going on, supported by the Arts Council, but most organisations undertaking this kind of work just don't have the opportunity to enter the spotlight in this way. That was an advantage as well.

We commissioned an evaluation that would document how the project progressed and its impact on all the partners and participants. We wanted the learning from the project to be shared widely to feed other similar initiatives, build a store of good practice and highlight the issues to government and others who have a stake in this important work. All part of the legacy.

The core idea was that young people aged 15–19 from Birmingham and the Black Country would train and perform with professionals from Birmingham Royal Ballet (BRB) in Kenneth Macmillan's production of Romeo and Juliet. Romeo and Juliet, it turned out, was an inspired choice of story:

star-crossed lovers, dysfunctional families, gang warfare, macho games, self-harm, drug abuse and knife crime; it had them all.

There were two phases. The first involved recruitment, enrolment, 'personal development training' and a follow-through programme from March 2005 to March 2006, concluding with a performance of work in progress at The Drum Theatre in Birmingham. 300 young people were recruited, 220 turned up for the Youth Intensive Training Courses, a four-day workshop led by Youth at Risk. Following this training, 150 committed themselves to a journey of personal

discovery, through dance and related arts, and 120 completed the first stage of this journey in March 2006.

At the beginning of the second phase the young people were asked whether or not they wished to continue. There followed an intensive period of work leading to the final performance of Romeo and Juliet. 85 young people signed up and 62 made it to the performance in September 2006, either on stage or backstage – exceeding the expectations of both Youth at Risk and BRB.

Of the young people who were involved and completed the second phase:

- 91% wanted to have further engagement in the performing arts;
- 50% were taking a course in the performing arts;
- 92% were back in education and training compared to 66% at the beginning of phase 1;

- 83% reported improved relationships with family or foster carers;
- 50% reported an improvement in anger management;
- 88% of the young people felt they had learned new skills.

The participants were able to use their experiences and achievements on the project as the basis for a BTEC. A total of 48 young people worked on their portfolios for Performing Arts either at BTEC certificate or diploma level during the course of the project. One respondent said that: 'My emotions kicked in after the performance. Maybe Ballet did change my life ... Now I feel I can stand up I can connect more emotionally to people.'

We are delighted that the initiative also continues to support young people through the Leaps and Bounds Trust, based in Dudley, delivering high quality arts opportunities alongside life coaching and personal development across the West Midlands, with many of the young people from Ballet Hoo! acting as mentors.

As I say, I've known Rod Morgan for a long time. He is an eminent criminologist and ex-Chair of the Youth Justice Board, who has become increasingly – and productively – involved in the area of youth arts, especially the arts and their impact on disadvantaged young people or young people at risk. He

brings to the area, as to this book, a wealth of experience, much wisdom, and a sound basis in sociological knowledge. Too often, commentaries on 'the arts and young people' are full of high-flown rhetoric, light on verifiable facts. Rod is just the person to take us beyond the rhetoric.

His 'insider's account' provides a very valuable counterpoint to the raw data and bare facts that emerged through the original evaluation. Clearly the project and the partnerships did not always run smoothly – the course of true love never did run smooth, after all – but what emerges is an extremely powerful and frank story of how the original ambition and vision came to be realised.

We are continuing to develop this strand of arts broadcasting with Channel 4 and others, investing in ambitious arts initiatives that seek to have an impact 'beyond the broadcast'. These include a new partnering of young people and orchestral work – with Diverse and the Hallé in Manchester – for transmission in 2010. Working with children and young people is central to

achieving the Arts Council's mission. It has to be. Engaging children and young people in the arts contributes to their initial education and development, and lays the foundation of a lifetime of involvement, participation and enjoyment.

One of our priorities continues to be encouraging and supporting artists and creative professionals to work directly in schools, informal learning centres, youth offending institutions and other places where young people are. I am so very glad that Ballet Hoo! happened during my time as Chair.

And as for those who would scoff at this approach to the arts and social inclusion – there are still a lot of them about, in my experience – I would only conclude "he jests at scars that never felt a wound".

SIR CHRISTOPHER
FRAYLING
CHAIR OF ARTS
COUNCIL ENGLAND

foreword

by Lord Phillips, Lord Chief Justice

TOO MUCH TO ASK?

The story of Leaps & Bounds

I get many requests from people who want to come to see me to discuss a wide variety of topics. When the topic is how to deal with the problem of keeping young people out of trouble they find that they are pushing at an open door.

The number of young people in this country who are receiving treatment as criminals is horrifying. We lock up more young people per head of population than any other country in Western Europe. Nor does this do much to reform the offenders who are locked up.

The majority of these are re-convicted within two years of release. This is why I always welcome visits from those, and there are many of them, who are involved in trying in one way or another to ensure that young people do not fall foul of the criminal justice system.

Thus it was that I welcomed one afternoon into my room at the Royal Courts of Justice, a large smiling man called Neil Wragg. He had asked to come to talk to me about an organisation he was running called 'Youth at Risk'. He spoke about his current project. This involved young and disadvantaged people in the Midlands, who were being

trained in order to participate with Birmingham Royal Ballet in a public performance of Prokofiev's Romeo and Juliet. Neil has a persuasive tongue, but I must admit to having to hide my scepticism about what seemed to me a pretty hare-brained scheme. None the less I agreed that, if I were free, I would go to see the proposed performance.

The invitation arrived. I was free. And so, on 28th September 2006 my wife and I set off for the Birmingham Hippodrome with the muted enthusiasm one normally feels at the prospect of going to see one's child performing a small part in a school play. What we saw was a superb performance in which we could not single out who was and who was not a professional ballet dancer.

The same was not true of the audience, made up of the friends and relatives of the young performers, who greeted the appearance of those they had come to see with the uninhibited enthusiasm that is usually reserved for the football stadium. At the end the curtain call lasted for a full twenty minutes, with many on the stage and in the audience in tears of emotion. It was the most memorable theatrical experience of my life.

Afterwards we watched the television series Ballet Hoo!, which gave us some idea of what the overall programme had involved, but left many questions unanswered, not least what happened to the young people involved after the dramatic day of the

performance. Kenneth Macmillan's widow, who had watched the performance, warned from the stage afterwards of the anti-climax that was bound to follow.

Rod Morgan's excellent book answers all our questions. It identifies the unique, and controversial, element in Youth at Risk's approach. This is the 'personal development training' which confronts a young person at the outset in intense group sessions of introspection which aim 'to create a lasting change in the mind-set, which will in turn lead participants to alter their actions and behaviours, enabling them to fulfil more of their potential'. The project then sets out to disclose to the participants that potential, usually undreamt of by them, for they are likely to have been repeatedly upbraided, in and out of school, as being useless. They are given a goal of artistic excellence and show that they are capable of achieving mastery.

Ballet Hoo! was all about creating self-respect, and this is the key to altering the lives of those who are drifting, disadvantaged and

often without a stable family background, in the direction of criminal behaviour. Critical is the establishment of a relationship with at least one adult who shows a belief in the worth and potential of the young person. Leaps & Bounds shows just what can be achieved by group endeavour to reach an achievement that is publicly recognised as outstanding. The value of the project was not merely that it transformed the lives of most of the young people involved, which it clearly did, albeit that in interview afterwards they were reluctant to concede this. It changed the lives and attitudes of many of the adults involved in the project. One of the ballet trainers involved remarked that she would probably have crossed the road to avoid some of the young people taking part, young people who were to become her friends. The project altered the attitude to dealing with young people of a number of local authorities and must have helped to sweep away prejudices, not only of those personally involved in the project, but of the huge television audience that followed its progress.

Have the effects been long lasting? Rod Morgan's book reassures us that they have. He includes accounts of interviews with a number of the young people involved and details of the follow-up research that has been conducted. Even those who dropped out of the programme have clearly benefited from their involvement in it. The book ends by telling us of two imaginative, and very different, projects now underway that have been inspired by Ballet Hoo!

Anyone who saw the performance in the Birmingham Hippodrome, whether in the flesh or on television, will enjoy and profit from this book. I hope that it will also inspire those with control of charitable or public funds to support the ventures inspired by Ballet Hoo!, for it demonstrates that the performance was not a 'one-off' moment of high drama, but the vindication of what must now be accepted as a proven method of transforming youth at risk.

LORD PHILLIPS
LORD CHIEF JUSTICE

Introduction

Rod Morgan

On Thursday 28th September 2006 my wife and I travelled from our home in the West Country to go to the theatre in Birmingham. It was a warm, late summer evening and we deliberately arrived early to attend a reception at the Green Room, opposite the Hippodrome Theatre.

'this book is about much more than that performance'

Rod Morgan

Although it was only 5.30 pm, we were not the first guests to arrive. The tables outside the restaurant were already crowded with people enjoying a pre-show drink. There was a definite buzz about the place and the mood was that something very special was about to take place.

Four to five hours later the street in front of the theatre was filled with a joyous crowd, of performers, producers, families and friends, whooping and hugging each other. Everyone knew that something very

special had taken place. Memorable... breathtaking... exhilarating.... truly wonderful... amazing achievement... wow man.... were the words on everybody's lips. The performers, the organizers and the audience drifted off in various directions, many to pre-arranged celebratory parties. We joined one such event and it was another two hours before my wife and I set off home down the M5 feeling almost light headed after all the excitement. What a pity, we said to each other, that our friends in the West

Country had not had the opportunity to share what we had witnessed.

But the opportunity did present itself. From 20th September to 7th October 2006, Channel 4 screened a series about the project entitled "Ballet Changed my Life: Ballet Hoo!" the climax of which was an hour and a half long resume of the spectacular Hippodrome performance. Sixty two 'disadvantaged' young people and a corps of dancers from the Birmingham Royal Ballet, accompanied by the Royal Ballet Sinfonia, had performed Prokofiev's Ballet, Romeo and Juliet (using an adaptation of Kenneth MacMillan's original choreography) before an audience of 2,500. The television audience of 4.2 million was such that Channel 4 subsequently repeated the programme and sparked a media frenzy of interest in dance as a means of reaching disadvantaged young people. It also made me an evangelist for the work underpinning the Ballet Hoo project.

During autumn 2006 I was still Chairman of the Youth Justice Board for England and Wales. My job often involved addressing audiences of magistrates and others with an interest in youth justice. One of my

constant refrains to such audiences is the British tendency to demonise young people; how foreigners observe that we seem to love our pets more than our children; how, as survey after survey shows, we spend so little time talking to and listening to our children compared to our European neighbours; how, as a state, we criminalise and lock up more young people per head of population than any other country in Western Europe; how so many of our young people are excluded from schools or do not attend them, reaching the age of 16 functionally illiterate and innumerate, with no qualifications. So, after the Channel 4 Ballet Hoo! series, I began asking my audiences if any of them

had seen the programmes. Half a dozen hands would typically be raised. I would ask: "What did you think?" And they would say things like: "I cried... those young people... amazing... so moving... fantastic achievement". Even now, anyone who visits me at home is liable to be asked if they saw the series and, if they haven't, I show them the Ballet Hoo! DVD produced by Diverse Productions.

That's one peg for this book: Ballet Hoo! – an astonishing, memorable performance one night, in Birmingham, in late September 2006. But this book is about much more than that performance. It follows a journey embarked on by more than 200 young people from the

West Midlands and a group of adults, employed by several very different organisations, who decided to do something extraordinary with and for those young people: to inspire them to realise the potential all of us have to live fulfilling, creative lives and to breathe life into some of the down-at-heel neighbourhoods from which many of the young people came. In documenting this journey I hope it might be replicated by others – all over Britain. For the performance at the Birmingham Hippodrome, in September 2006, represents just a staging post on a continuing journey. It was wonderfully important but it was only part of the story, and certainly not the end of it. In Dudley, in the Black

Country, there is now a registered Trust, Leaps & Bounds, organising yet more inspirational journeys for young people of which Ballet Hoo! was a sort of one-off, master-stroke; a probably never-to-be-repeated prototype. Leaps & Bounds is the creation of Dudley Metropolitan Borough Council . The Trust is working with Youth at Risk, a national charity devoted, as its name suggests, to the personal development of young people who for various reasons are marginalised. Indeed it was Youth at Risk's Chief Executive, Neil Wragg, who first put the idea for Ballet

Hoo! to Andrew Sparke, Dudley's Chief Executive. By that stage, as we shall see, Neil had already developed a partnership with other organisations, Diverse Productions, Channel 4, and Birmingham Royal Ballet, who wanted to stage a dance and personal development project for young people if a local authority partner could be found.

It is important to say what this book is not. It is not an academic work or a research report. It is not an impartial evaluation of the effectiveness of dance or arts-related education. It is the story

of a project. Readers will not find within its pages detailed data on the numbers of children and young people at risk by virtue of family breakdown, their exclusion from school, their precocious sexual activity, their early use of alcohol or illegal drugs, and so on. Neither will they find statistics about child poverty and the widening gulf between the haves and the have nots in contemporary Britain, the prevalence of youth crime, the carrying of knives, or the numbers of children and young people criminalised or locked up. This book has a different purpose. It is

aimed at those who commission such programmes: arts organisations, local authorities, charities and community groups, interested in an insiders' account of an imaginative, creative venture which proved inspirational and fulfilling for almost all of those young people and staff touched by it.

This is the story of a project and the lives of the people involved. In the course of its telling important lessons emerge: lessons about the complexities of partnership working; about imbalances of power; about the misunderstandings that arise when organisations representing very different worlds, try to speak with one voice in order to achieve a common purpose; and about how different participating partners can support each other so that the gains are greater than the contributory parts.

Be assured this story is worth telling for, as we shall see, the rewards are very great.

Rod Morgan.

chapter 1

'a daft idea'

The seed is sown

On 17th October, 2003, Andrew Sparke, Chief Executive of Dudley council welcomed Neil Wragg of Youth At Risk, a national charity, into his office. Neil had asked for a meeting to sell a programme in development training for senior public sector staff.

They soon discovered they had both worked for the London Borough of Enfield during the `80s and early `90s where they had taken part in a similar ground breaking personal development programme. Andrew could see real value in what Neil was selling. The problem was that he did not have available resources to invest in such staff training.

Nevertheless he quickly became interested in another idea Neil appeared to pull out of his back

pocket. Neil explained that he was looking for a local authority in the West Midlands to join a partnership with Youth At Risk (YAR), Birmingham Royal Ballet (BRB) and Diverse Productions, which makes programmes for Channel 4. The local authority role would be to identify, fund and support young people at risk who would engage in a personal development programme and learn to dance sufficiently well to put on a public performance, all of

which might be the subject of a television series. This fascinating idea caught Andrew's imagination and in the weeks that followed he invested substantial personal energy in getting his fellow Chief Executive's in the West Midlands interested in the project and subsequently securing the contractual commitments which would make the idea financially and operationally possible.

The genesis of the idea and the man who sold it

The dance element of the project was not originally Neil Wragg's idea. Indeed when it was first suggested to him, Neil, ex-army and with substantial experience of working with young people from traditional working class areas, admits he was taken aback and laughed. The idea was Roy Ackerman's, a Director of Diverse Productions, the film-making company with whom Neil had built up a firm working partnership over several years.

Neil Wragg is a formidable man in every sense. Physically very large, with an engaging smile and solid Derbyshire accent, he has built up a substantial reputation in youth work over twenty years and counts as personal friends some very powerful and influential people in both the public sector and the commercial world. Yet he can talk the language of the streets and has endearing laddish qualities. He doesn't put on airs. He makes friends and influences people and is not afraid to knock on anyone's door. Neil comes from a rather unconventional, bohemian home background, didn't do well at school and to some extent lived, as an adolescent, in the shadow of an older, more academically successful brother.

He liked sport, and when he was old enough, he signed on and spent three years as a Tank Regiment squaddie.

At 21 he left the army, and uncertain what he wanted to do, he took a series of jobs in London working with the homeless in street and housing projects. He started as a community service volunteer in a London night shelter for down-and-outs and subsequently worked for the Peter Bedford Trust providing support for people coming out of mental hospitals. From this he went on to work in a residential home with what were then termed Educational Sub Normal (ESN) young people before working at CentrePoint.

During this period Neil had formative experiences which helped shape his subsequent commitment, understanding and ambition in youth work. A young man who Neil turned away while working at CentrePoint was murdered by the serial killer Dennis Neilsen. This experience profoundly changed his thinking. He decided that the night shelter approach wasn't good enough; he had to get into some activity that made it less likely that young, vulnerable people would find themselves in desperate need of something like a night shelter. It was for him not unlike the parable of the man who is fishing a river into which he frequently feels impelled to dive to save drowning bodies that come floating down, but who eventually decides he has to walk upstream to find out who is pushing these people in.

So in the mid 80s Neil went to Enfield, working as a local authority community development worker before qualifying as a social worker. He then opened a community centre for black youths and was shocked at the level of police racism towards his clients.

The manager of the local authority-owned shopping centre where Neil's youth centre was based caused him further problems by lobbying for the youth centre to be closed, arguing that since it had opened, the incidence of crime in the shopping centre had rocketed, which he attributed to black youths frequenting the area. When the claim was repeated at a public meeting, Neil was accused of lying. He was

The genesis of Ballet Hoo! lies in the connection between Neil Wragg and Roy Ackerman, the television director.

now in deep trouble, and was asked to substantiate his charge, for which, at that stage, he had no firm evidence. With senior police assistance he was subsequently able to prove that the crime rate in the shopping centre had, in fact, gone down.

This experience taught Neil some critical lessons: prejudice and injustice has to be confronted; vulnerable young people must be stood up for; and evidence has to be collected to defend good programmes.

Neil Wragg was still working for the London Borough of Enfield when he met Roy Ackerman. Roy was already interested in YAR's work and when Neil commissioned YAR to run a community programme in Enfield, the result was a 40 minute

Channel 4 programme entitled Tough Love.

The programme was screened in 1994 as part of a series of programmes called Cutting Edge. It attracted a lot of attention and created quite a stir. It was well received, but shocked many youth service practitioners. The critics were taken aback by the intensity of the group process which YAR uses; young participants being encouraged to stand up within the group and talk about feelings and experiences which can be highly emotional. A less visible outcome of Tough Love was that Neil and Roy developed a professional friendship which has continued since Neil became YAR's Chief Executive in 1994. Roy has advised YAR about, among other things,

their media strategy.

Roy Ackerman's Diverse Productions went on to make two very successful programmes for Channel 4: Operatunity and Musicality. In Operatunity, the theme was a search for unknown persons to sing alongside established international opera stars in Rigoletto with the English National Opera at the Coliseum, and the series won a clutch of awards. In Musicality the process involved unknown singers and dancers being given the opportunity to star in a West End musical, Chicago.

The core idea behind the programmes has since become a fashionable TV genre – the proposition that apparently ordinary people can, if given the opportunity, achieve apparently

extraordinary things, and that many of us have much greater potential to achieve things than typically we realise. This same idea lies at the heart of YAR's philosophy.

Roy had the idea of taking this approach further with ballet, and casually suggested to Neil Wragg that the concept be given a twist. What about a ballet project involving YAR? Neil had some familiarity with the 'high culture' arts world, but he had never been to watch first class ballet and says that his immediate reaction was that Roy was crazy. For people not from privileged backgrounds ballet appeared to Neil to have all the wrong characteristics and connotations – elitist, precious, traditional, expensive :- people prancing about in tights on a stage

with lots of gay innuendo, not exactly the tough world of urban gangster rap. But one night in early 2004 he accepted Roy's invitation to go to Covent Garden to see a performance of Prokofiev's Romeo and Juliet. His initial reaction confirmed his earlier thoughts and prejudices: it was all about "people in tuxedos and being in the club." He thought "we can't do this... the kids we work with, and I, don't belong here." But as the performance progressed Neil recalls that he got into it and the experience was for him "like a light bulb being switched on".

It wasn't just the extraordinary athleticism and professionalism of the dancers, or even the obvious relevance of Shakespeare's story of feuding families and street fighting. At the point in

the story where, as Neil remembers it, Juliet's father says to her "You keep going out with that guy and you're out the house", he suddenly twigged that Roy's concept could work. Indeed it was exactly because the world of professional ballet was in one sense so far removed from the world of the young people with whom YAR wishes to work - a world of self-evident dedication, professionalism, excellence and mastery, as opposed to a world frequently characterised by lack of discipline, failure, alienation and hopelessness - that Neil began to think, ballet could be a learning bridge that YAR might use. The Ballet, Romeo and Juliet seemed capable of powerfully encapsulating human relationships and emotions which are familiar and universal and could also be

the confrontational mirror of excellence held up to address what is often the young people's sense of personal failure. It might be the device that would pose the question: If you can learn to do some of this, imagine what else you can do!

Neil Wragg's imagination was fired. He thought the performance at Covent Garden was fantastic and the more he learned about ballet thereafter convinced him that this was a scheme that could work.

YAR, Diverse Productions and Channel 4 reached an agreement for a programme series after which it was a question of forging a partnership with a leading ballet company and finding a local authority which would sponsor some young people.

In the months that followed it became apparent, despite the fact that the Chief Executive at Covent Garden was keen, that a project involving the company and Diverse Productions wasn't on, at least not at the time. The BBC had exclusive television rights to Covent Garden's productions and Diverse Productions was working with Channel 4. There was intense competition between the BBC and Channel 4 and this was no-go territory. So the idea was born that an approach be made to Birmingham Royal Ballet (BRB). This proposition greatly appealed to Neil, a Midlander who thinks that far too much media coverage is London-centric.

Roy Ackerman set up a meeting with, Derek Purnell, the then Chief Executive of

BRB and the Artistic Director, David Bintley. The meeting went well. The BRB people were enthusiastic. What Neil Wragg now needed was one or more local authority partners and a group of disadvantaged young people. He did his homework.

BRB receives significant funding from Birmingham City Council. Birmingham was therefore the obvious local authority partner. Moreover, BRB wanted Birmingham as their local authority partner: ideally as the lead partner if there were to be several local authorities involved. Their education department saw the Ballet Hoo project as an extension of their existing, mainstream, rather successful, community engagement programme with the City Council. Neil Wragg,

however, did not. In his judgement the Ballet Hoo project would, and should, be different. Neil also knew that the Council might prove a sticky wicket for him. Birmingham is a very big local authority and, at the time, had something of a Big Brother reputation. The authority was said by other local authorities to be messy to deal with. Youth at Risk is a small voluntary organisation. Neil needed clear, top level backing and firm local authority resolve. He doubted he could get it from Birmingham. At which point he thought of Dudley, with whose Chief Executive he already had a meeting planned.

Neil knew that the Dudley chief executive, Andrew Sparke, was engaged in a culture change programme and wished to develop his

senior managers. He knew all this because he meets a good many chief executives and learns, on the grapevine, where progressive things are happening and, by contrast, where resistance is likely to be encountered. YAR had just completed a training programme for senior staff in Leicestershire, one of the pilot areas for development of the new childrens' trusts. So he had his ear close to the network and was alert to those local authorities and chief executives interested in developing innovative ways of working with young people.

It follows that when they met Neil did not, despite appearances, pull the Ballet Hoo proposal from his back pocket as an after-thought. He had already set his sights

on Andrew and Dudley for the realisation of the project.

The Local Authority Chief Executive's Vision

Andrew Sparke is an energetic, creative, local authority chief executive . He is seriously committed to the Black Country in which he has worked for nine years. He likes the people, lives in Stourbridge in the heart of his patch and takes an active part in a large range of local affairs. He is politically and managerially astute and Neil Wragg's idea for a major, high profile youth project struck a chord with him because he immediately grasped that it could light a beacon for his local authority. But his administrative and financial experience also told him that the project was not one that Dudley council could

entertain alone. If it was going to happen he would have to engineer a collaborative enterprise and put his personal weight behind it. But Andrew, like all effective chief executives, likes the entrepreneurial aspect of his role and was willing to invest the effort required.

Dudley, and the Black Country, has an above average proportion of young people who are unemployed and who, in the dispiriting Whitehall jargon of the day, are NEETS, that is, aged 16-24 and not in education, employment or training. Andrew was concerned by the substantial proportion of these young people aged 16-18 who he knew were not being reached by Dudley's rather traditional, youth club-centred, youth service. He knew that a high proportion of Dudley's youth service budget was tied up in physical facilities which were often geographically in the wrong place. He wanted a push for more outreach work with these young people who, as one research report after another has emphasised, are, if not positively engaged, more than likely destined to join the ranks of the long-term adult unemployed and, in a

significant number of cases, to become persistent, adult career criminals. The knock-on financial consequences of failing this generation of young people, of leaving them with few prospects of successfully entering the labour market, are huge. Reducing the size of the NEET generation is fairly obviously a task best tackled with much younger children. But what Neil was proposing seemed like an attractive lifeline for some young people before it was almost too late for them.

There was another dimension to Andrew's thinking. Andrew is honest enough to admit that the prospect of assisting a relatively small handful of Dudley young people was not his most immediate consideration. He saw Neil's project as a strategic device which, longer term, could achieve much more and, ultimately, might indeed benefit the young people of Dudley more widely. He had two thoughts in mind. He was conscious that decision making in his local authority, though effective in some ways, was too hierarchical and top down. He wanted to plant a project which would be visible and inspirational to his staff with the potential to

stimulate more grass-roots, creative schemes for tackling the relatively intractable, unpromising futures facing a large number of Dudley's young people. Andrew was also conscious that many staff who work with socially excluded, troubled and troublesome young people are themselves ground down, with low expectations of their clients' potential and what it is possible to do with them. He was looking to change the whole culture of his local authority and its staff. He literally wanted a device which would shake up his professional youth service staff and get them thinking about different ways in which they might more effectively do their job as teams, responding to the needs of their more hard-to-reach clients.

He discussed Neil's proposition with his senior colleagues and they decided that for Dudley the project was not too big a risk. The worst that could happen was that they might be made to look naive or a little foolish on television. Here was a real opportunity to put Dudley on the map. The possibility of Dudley's young people being seen nationally on TV participating in a ground-breaking project of this nature was just too good an opportunity to pass up.

Andrew understood why Birmingham might be more lukewarm about the project. He appreciated that Birmingham, because of its size, regional importance and greater prestige, would be less motivated to go for an initiative which many would judge risky. He knew that Birmingham already attracted a lot of media interest for its economic regeneration and other programmes. Put crudely, Birmingham didn't need the project in the same way that Dudley and the Black Country did. But he concluded that the four Black Country local authorities – Dudley, Sandwell, Walsall and Wolverhampton – combined, would be sufficiently large to

carry the project even if Birmingham could not be persuaded to join them. He gave Neil Wragg a positive response and set about establishing a consortium of chief executives willing to buy into the project. Neil was impressed by Andrew's resolve and dynamism, though he anticipated difficulties ahead. Neil thought the upper echelons of Birmingham Royal Ballet might resent Dudley becoming the lead local authority, in particular their education department who might see the project as outreach business as usual. Neil knew they would have to embrace a different approach.

When they were approached Andrew's fellow Black Country chief executives largely shared his vision,

though they were not always able, either at that stage or later, to carry their senior management colleagues with them. But by January 2005, only a matter of weeks later, Andrew had a contract signed by four local authorities. In the event Walsall, which was going through a sticky patch with the Audit Commission, concluded that the project could not be a priority for them: they were subject to direct government intervention at the time and did not sign up. But somewhat surprisingly Birmingham, the biggest, most prestigious, player did. As things turned out, the difficulties of working with Birmingham City Council, anticipated by Neil Wragg, proved correct. The manner in which the project was made operational in

Birmingham turned out to be very different from that in the Black Country, an issue to which we shall return in the next chapter.

The Project Director: in at the deep end

Keith Horsfall is in his mid 50s and has had a long career in music teaching. He's a trustee of the National Association of Youth Orchestras and prior to becoming Project Director was the deputy manager of Dudley Performing Arts, the local authority's programme for youth music and community engagement in the arts. No one in Dudley, where Keith had worked for more than twenty years, had more experience of organising large scale musical and other arts events for young people than Keith. He identifies with and likes young people and throughout his teaching and organising career has opted to work in relatively deprived areas with less advantaged young people. Since taking responsibility for Dudley's Arts Centre in Netherton in 2000 he had, with the benefit of various sources of funding, transformed it into 'the place to be'.

It is well known that Keith is a man who likes challenges and rises to them. He is also a man who tells it like it is. An enthusiast who hates red-tape, he's a fast talking, bloody-minded maverick, which is possibly why Dudley's community arts structure and music service in particular survived the cuts and devolution of funding to schools which saw off so many other local

authority community music and arts organisations in the 1990s. Keith describes himself as affable and his management style as light-touch. But, as he says, when the programme is something which he feels passionate about and he's pushed into a corner – "then I don't care what I say to whom!" It was natural for Andrew Sparke, to look in Keith's direction when the ballet proposal came up.

When Keith first heard about the ballet project through an emailed 'message of the day' - 'is anybody out there interested in this?' - he liked the sound of it. It was said to be about 'disadvantaged' kids and would involve teaching them to dance alongside a personal development programme. It seemed just the ticket for him. The email referred to a Co-ordinator role in the Black Country and Keith inferred from this that there would be an equivalent co-ordinator from Birmingham, with shared project leadership. He thought this could be a recipe for disaster. However, if there was to be an overall project co-ordinator, then he would definitely be interested. He chose to take the bull by the horns and phone Andrew to express his interest.

Nobody else had put their head above the parapet to tackle the project and Andrew was keen to see Keith as soon as possible to persuade him to run the project for him. He invited Keith to meet and Keith duly attended Andrew's office on 6th October 2004.

Keith had never worked directly to Andrew before, though in the natural course of events he'd met his ultimate boss two or three times. After hearing further details about the project, Keith asked whether there was a project plan and was assured there was. Then he, being Keith, asked whether there were any working restrictions to be placed on the role of overall Project Co-ordinator, the job he now knew he was being offered. For example, would he and his staff have to complete

signing-in sheets if they worked the odd, late hours he knew would be involved. Andrew assured him, not. He placed no restrictions on him other than the usual ones: child protection, (which had to be water-tight), and standard audit controls. He was not to do anything which would get the authority into trouble. Other than that, he had to make it happen. In fact, on subsequently seeing the provisional project plan Keith was convinced it was undeliverable and would have to be altered. But these details were yet to come. When was he to start? 1st November, he was told, in three weeks time.

Keith left the Chief Executive's office and went down to the arts centre where he was due to do a presentation that evening with his boss. He told his boss he had his services for another three weeks and then he'd be off. He'd got his chance to be number one on a roller-coaster project that would continue until the Hippodrome performance on 28 September 2006 and, as things turned out, was not to end there.

During the summer and autumn of 2007
I went up to Birmingham and the Black
Country to meet some of the Ballet Hoo
graduates individually.

Stories of the Young People

This is the first of seven individual portraits. In almost every
case I talked to the young people in their own homes, or
where they were currently living. There is a distinction. Home
implies a degree of permanence, settled-in-ness, having one's
things around one. Some of the young people were not in
that situation. They were on the move, sofa-surfing, camping.
Whatever their situations, the locations were where they
invited me to come, where I found them. Being on their home
territory meant I sometimes met parents, siblings, partners or
friends, albeit only in passing.

In the first instance I tape
recorded what I was told
and then made it into as
coherent a story as I've been
able to tell; not precisely in
their own words but told as
faithfully as possible.

In some cases the stories
are not as complete as I
heard them. The identities of
each of the young people
has been disguised. But
there can be no disguising
most of them, at least not as
far as colleagues close to
the Ballet Hoo! project are
concerned, or even those
who saw the TV series. So,
where the young people

have concluded, subsequent
to our meeting, that part of
their recorded story could be
hurtful to someone close to
them, they have taken a red
pen to my account, which is
wise of them.
One last introductory
comment. What follows is
what I was told. I have made
no attempt to verify
anything. Some things may
not be true or may only
partly be true. Recollections
can be faulty. We all re-
invent ourselves, constantly.
But on the grounds that
whatever is recollected and
told, right or wrong,
becomes part of what one

is, the accounts that follow –
where they say they have
come from, where they are
now and where they think
they might go – are
important. They have the
ring of truth and it is clear
that for each and every one
of them the Ballet Hoo!
project has been critically
important in their lives.

D's Story

D is elusive. After several weeks of trying I eventually get hold of his mobile phone number. He wants to meet me. He suggests that I come to his Mum's address in Wolverhampton.

But two hours before our appointment I get a message suggesting that I come to his girlfriend's council flat instead. The complex of flats is grim, close to the centre of Wolverhampton on the road to Wednesbury. The deck-access building is four stories high, surrounded by a litter-strewn, concrete wasteland. Across the Wednesbury Road is a row of well-lit fast-food shops.

The stairwell smells of urine. A group of youths stand at the far end of the walkway. There is no answer to D's doorbell. Loud, thumping music is coming from next door. Standing there, waiting, apparently without purpose, makes me feel awkward. I am conscious that I look distinctly out of place – old, white, grey-bearded, carrying a briefcase. But after a few minutes D appears at the far end of the walkway, wearing a hoodie, smiling broadly,

waving a greeting. He lets me in. The flat is a 60s maisonette. At the top of the uncarpeted stairs is a small barely furnished living room. D sits in an arm-chair and I sit on the sofa. This is where he lives with his girlfriend. She works for Coral, the bookmakers and is not home yet. D makes me feel immediately comfortable. We start to talk

I'm 18. I've got an older brother and a sister. My parents were both in the army. So when I was a child we moved around a lot – Salisbury in Wiltshire, Northern Ireland, Market Drayton, Germany, Huddersfield. I was about five or six years old when my parents left the forces. We lived in Huddersfield then and moved to Wolverhampton when I was 11. I went to Wednesfield High School. It was different from the secondary school I went to in Huddersfield. To begin with I felt a bit of an

outsider because from the way I spoke I was obviously not from round here. Also, it wasn't the secondary school I wanted to go to. I wanted to go to Heath Park in Wolverhampton. The other kids I'd got to know went to Heath Park. But my Mum didn't want me to go there: she thought Wednesfield High was a better school.

It was OK to begin with. I went. I was in the volleyball and football teams. I was into all the sports and I was good at sports, particularly football. I got good grades. I was in the top set for everything. But in the end it wasn't a success. When I was 13 I got excluded and things went downhill after that.

I was on my way to school by bus and another boy from my school spat a mouthful of cheese crisps at me. I hit him with a backhand. I didn't mean to, but I popped his nose. I took him with me off the bus to the hospital so that his broken nose got seen to. But the school excluded me. I said 'What for? I took him to the hospital'.

"But the school excluded me anyway"

and I was reprimanded by the police, because the boy's father reported me. There was a governors' meeting to decide whether I could come back. They decided I was trouble despite the fact that I'd never been in trouble before and I'd been in the top set for everything. My parents were angry about it all. They wanted to write to the Express and Star because to begin with the school were going to expel me. I shouldn't have retaliated but this boy deliberately spat at me. He and his mates thought it was funny. I got excluded for two and a

half weeks and after that everything went to pan. I got chucked off things at school. I was angry about the way I was treated. There was quite a large group of black kids in my year, though the school was mostly white. And whenever there was a fight I tended to get blamed, even if I wasn't there. I'd been labelled as a troublemaker and I think the fact that I was black was a factor. I was OK with other kids in the playground and elsewhere. There it was great. People didn't trouble me. It was the teachers and the managers of the teachers, they were the people that got me into trouble. They destroyed me. And so my attitude changed. I couldn't be bothered. It

didn't seem to matter what I did, I was going to get into trouble anyway. I got excluded several times. Once for chucking a snowball, and I hadn't chucked no snowball. Once they excluded me for something that happened in school and I wasn't even in school at the time: I was at the doctors'.

There were some teachers who helped me – quite a few really. Because they could see what was going on. They would tell me that if I was accused of causing trouble that I should say this, and this, and this, and stick up for myself. But the school put me on a mentor. I was OK in art and IT and things like that, where I knew what

MUCH ASK **THE LEAPS & BOUNDS STORY**

22

to do. But for maths they put me in the top set, and I'm not top set maths. They give me too hard questions to answer: I can't do top set maths. I said to them: 'I'm hopeless at maths. I can't do it. I don't understand. Why you put me in top set maths?' I felt I was set up to fail. The same with English. Don't get me wrong, I'm OK at English. But I'm not top set – I'm more in the middle. So when we did Shakespeare and things like that, I couldn't understand all of it and told the teacher. And the teacher would say 'You have to understand it, everyone else understands it.' And I would say 'Put me in another class then. This is too hard for me. I don't understand it.' But they kept me in the class. When it came to the GCSEs I got five passes. I got Bs in Business Studies and Art and a C in IT. But I failed in Maths and English. And by then I'd been excluded about four times. Once I was excluded for standing at a fight. Not for fighting, but standing at a fight. They said I shouldn't have been there. In my last year at school, a few days before the end of the term, I was told not to come any more. Don't come back, they said. That was the end of my time at Wednesbury High School.

I got a job as an assistant manager at British Home Stores. I did things in the office: checking the stock; customer service; cash flow; things like that. I worked for them for about a year. I'd had no more trouble with the police since the reprimand when I was 13 and I was still living with my parents. I won't say that I hadn't done anything – smoking weed, things like that. And I'd watched other people do things –stealing things – but I hadn't done stuff like that myself and I hadn't been arrested. But then, when I was 17, while I was working for British Home Stores, I was arrested for a stupid armed robbery of four people. We took – well I didn't take – but we took two handbags and credit cards from four people in the street. There were three of us. One of them was my older brother. It was an armed robbery because my brother had a knife. My brother's not been a big influence in my life, but he's been in trouble from when he was eight or nine and he's been constantly in court since he was about 11.

He's been to prison about eight times. In fact he's institutionalised: it's the life he knows. But that evening I was bored and he said 'Do you want to come out with me?' and I said 'OK'. I didn't know what he was going to do. I didn't know he was going to rob someone. He held the knife and said to me 'Take the bag'. And I did. It was crazy. We got caught almost immediately and I gave myself up straight away. There was a police helicopter looking for us and an armed squad. I came before the magistrates' court and I was remanded in custody, though later I got bail. [At this point D's girlfriend, Jessica, comes home and we introduce ourselves. Someone calls her on her mobile phone and she goes to another room.] Everyone, including my Mum, said I wouldn't go to prison because I didn't have a criminal record: 'You won't get that' everyone told me. But at Wolverhampton Crown Court the judge gave me a two years DTO [Detention and Training Order].

They sent me to Brinsford YOI near Wolverhampton. I thought it was dreadful to begin with, but you get used to it. Then they sent me to Thorn Cross open YOI near

Warrington. I did really well there. I was the first juvenile to play in their football team. I worked outside. I did a team leaders course. I led a team skiing outside. They wanted me to stay up there. I was trusted. Then while I was there, this guy called Ian [Ian Wright, the Ballet Hoo Co-ordinator for Wolverhampton] came to see me. He asked if I would like to do this ballet project. And I said 'Yeah. I like a challenge. I'll do anything. Put me in for it.' So he did and the governor released me early on a tag to do it. I'd never done any dancing before.

So I came back to Wolverhampton and went to this hall where they were seeing people for this dance project and there I was interviewed by Ian Wright. They said this project was for guys and girls but [laughs with glee] there was only girls there apart from me. I told them that my three life goals were: get a good job straight away; get back in the football team; and not give any stress to my Mum again.

I did the four day intensive course at the beginning. It was alright. It made sense to me. They made us think more. What do you want to do? What do you want to be? How do you want to do it? Where are you going from here? All that was really important to me because I'd just come out of prison. But they made it stretch on too long. They could have narrowed it down to two days. But it helped. I had a sort of idea of where I wanted to go, but nothing precise. Anyway, I got into the project and things went well. And though I had some difficulty getting work I didn't get into trouble again. I was living mostly with Jessica now and she made sure that I got up and went to the

project sessions on time. [Jessica joins us at this point and confirms how good theproject was for D and how she made sure he went to everything he was able to.] And everything went well until the incident with my Dad.

On New Year's Day 2006 [D's birthday is 1 January] my Dad rang me up from London – I don't know what he was doing down there, something to do with work I think – he asked me to give a message to my Mum. He didn't wish me a Happy Birthday or anything and I was supposed to be going out. It was all going off. But I went to see my Mum for him and she wished me a Happy Birthday and asked me if my Dad had. I said no. And he never gave me anything either. This all got into my head. I could have had a better relationship with my

Dad, but I wouldn't say it was bad. But I didn't like the way he took the piss out of my Mum. Because a bit later he sold the family car. I don't know why. He just sold it. And my Mum in those days never used a bus and she worked in West Bromwich. She needed the car to get to work. I was round there a few days later and my sister had just moved up to Huddersfield and my Mum needed to get to West Bromwich. So I said I'd go with her on the bus. I had no money, so he gave me money to take my Mum on the bus and we got to West Brom. And then we got home and neither my Mum or I had had anything to eat. And when we got in my Dad said to us: 'What's for dinner?'. So I said 'What planet are you on?' She'd been to work and hadn't had anything to eat and now he's expecting her to get food for

him and she's got to go back to work. So I looked in the cupboard and there was no food. I said 'What the hell's going on?' I had no money so I decided I was going to ask my Dad for the phone back that I'd given him as a Christmas present earlier. I suppose it was a sort of joke because I don't know what I was going to do with the phone, but I asked my Mum first if I was right to do that, and she said yes. So I said to my Dad: 'Can I have the phone back?' And he, like Superman, picked up a chair and threw it at me. Then he rushed at me and got his hands round my neck shouting 'I'm going to kill you'.

I'd had set-tos with my Dad before, but never serious fighting. Because he's my Dad, and you're sort of scared to do anything to your Dad: you just take the

beating. But this time I said 'Are you sure you want to kill me?' and he said 'Yes'. So I got away from him and went to the kitchen, got a knife and started chasing him round the house. I said to him 'You're not working. You know that I've not been working long and haven't got much because I've just come out. You've got a mortgage to pay. And now you seem to be doing everything you can to get my Mum to quit her job.' I stabbed him in the chest. It was serious because the blade broke and I just had the wooden handle. But by that stage I'd completely lost it. My Mum was trying to drag me off, but I was still going. He was shouting 'Get out of my house', and I was shouting 'It's not your house, it's my Mum's house'.

I left and came back at about two in the morning

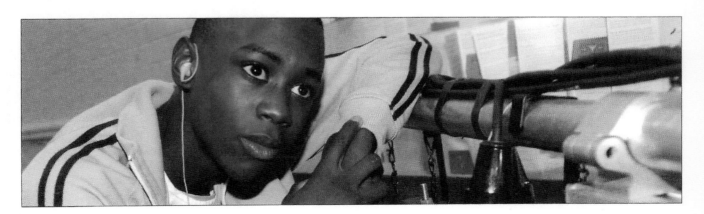

with some food for my Mum. My Dad wasn't there: he'd gone. So we went to bed. My Mum works nights, but she wasn't going to work that night. Then at about four in the morning someone knocks at the front door. I told my Mum to leave it. I said if it's my Dad, he's got his own key. But she opened the door and an armed police squad rushed in as if I was a mass murderer. They took me off in my boxer shorts.

I got bail even though I was initially charged with attempted murder. I think it was because I had a job, I was involved in the project and I was working as a volunteer at a legal advice centre. I'd had a series of jobs since I'd come out of Thorn Cross. I was on track. Ian (his Project Co-ordinator) spoke up for me and my Mum spoke up for me. I

admitted I'd stabbed my Dad but I didn't plead guilty to attempted murder. He'd attacked me. If he hadn't attacked me nothing would have happened. He's bigger and stronger than me. He's built like a bulldozer. I said I'd acted in self-defence. But in the end I pleaded guilty to grievous bodily harm. And everyone said that because I'd been to prison before I was looking at five years. Everyone said that. And while I was on bail I couldn't live in or go to the house. I was banned from the whole area. I was waiting for a flat at the time, but it hadn't come through so I lived with my sister for a bit and then with Jessica.

The dance project helped me enormously at the time. I didn't have a life coach. Everyone else did, but I worked with Ian and he came everywhere with me

and helped me. I didn't talk about what was happening to me to people in the project and even though it was mentioned in the TV series most people in the project didn't know about it at the time. I was sentenced in May 2006 at Wolverhampton Crown Court, four months before the Hippodrome performance. Ian and my Mum spoke up for me again and, contrary to the sentence that everyone told me I was going to get, I got probation with various conditions that I go to groups and that sort of thing. I'd finished my licence at that stage, but now I had to start all over again. And I couldn't get jobs now. I've never had a proper job since. I used to be able to get them, but now I can't. I can only get casual, low paid stuff now.
The Ballet Hoo people were

great. Though things have been a bit tough since the project finished it has helped me, though I've always been energetic and willing to have a go at things. [Jessica comes in again – she says " It's definitely made him more confident in himself. He always used to say he would do things, but you could tell he wasn't that confident. Now he's really willing to do it and is confident he can about it."]

I was going to be Lord Capulet in the final performance. But I had problems getting to some of the rehearsals towards the end because of other things that were going on at the time. I had to go to probation groups, for example. I think I was regarded as very important within the project because when I was at a rehearsal people didn't mess about as much. I motivated them. I

got on with everyone and people said that the atmosphere was more positive when I was there. At the Hippodrome I played four different parts in the crowd scenes. They said I learned the steps really quickly. That evening was great. My Mum and Jessica were there. It was great. Afterwards people who saw me on the TV congratulated me and told me I had to do more of that.

I get a bit dispirited now over not having a decent job because there's no easy solution to my position. I've done all the courses they ask you to do. Things like Steps to Work, how to do an interview, how to fill out an application form, all that. I know all that stuff like the back of my hand. I've done it all, several times. But all I get

is occasional agency work. As soon as they see my record they don't offer me an interview. I've told Ali [Ali Reilly of the Leaps & Bounds follow-on project] I want to help with one of the projects they're doing now.

What's difficult is that I graft, but I get nothing and I've got nothing. I see people round here who do drugs and stuff and get loads of money for doing nothing. They go out and get a new car and stacks of new clothes, just like that. It gets to you because you can't do any of those things and they can. You don't want to go down that road because it ends in disaster. Don't get me wrong, I've done a bit of that in the past. But I don't want to do it now. You can't really spend the money because you're not working – so where's it coming from? You end up destroying everything or getting stabbed or something like that. There's no point to it. I want a decent job. I want to do something worthwhile. And it's bad round here. There's nothing for the kids to do. There used to be an astro-turf pitch at the back of these flats where we could play football. But they took it all away and just concreted it over. Now there's nothing. Just a hard surface on which it would be dangerous to play football. I always got on with my Mum and I still do. My relationship with my Dad is so-so. He's not aggressive with me as he used to be. We can talk. He's not hostile. In fact my relationship with him is better now than it was before even though he could have stopped the GBH case against me. And I'm with Jessica – we've been together for about three years now. She supports

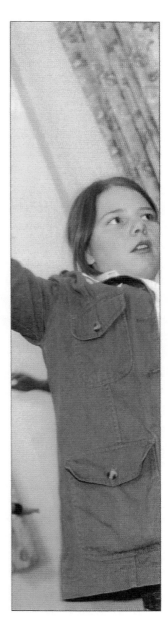

me. I think if I stay positive thing's will eventually come right.

After I switch the tape-recorder off saying that I really have to go now, D protests that he's only covered the first instalment of his story. He wants to talk more. He sees me down the stairs to the front door. The deck corridor is dark and a group of youths are messing about with a football a few doors away. He checks with me that the car is where I parked it. And when, having got to my car, I look up, he's still standing there, making sure that I get away OK. He waves as I drive off towards the centre of Wolverhampton and south towards the M5.

chapter 2

'it'll never work'

Chance Encounter and First Blood

In the late afternoon of 18th November 2004 I arrived at a rather smart, residential conference centre at Chartridge, near Chesham in Buckinghamshire. I was then the relatively new Chairman of the Youth Justice Board and had been persuaded by Neil Wragg to participate in a 24 hour Immersion course so that I could personally experience YAR's methods.

I was aware that his organisation possibly had much to offer the young people for whom I was most concerned: those who had fallen foul of the law or were at risk of doing so. I knew and trusted the judgement of one or two of the people sitting on Neil's Advisory Board – Breidge Gadd, formerly Chief Probation Officer, Northern Ireland, David Ramsbotham, formerly Chief Inspector of Prisons and Michael Zander, Professor of Law at the London School of Economics. But I also had respected friends who doubted YAR's approach. Now I had the opportunity to see for myself.

As I was looking for the entrance to the centre, I bumped into Keith Horsfall, the newly appointed Co-ordinator for the Ballet Hoo! project.

I don't remember how Keith introduced himself, but whatever he said it didn't register. I knew nothing about his project and assumed that, like myself, he was at Chartridge just to learn, dispassionately, what Youth at Risk was all about. In fact, of course, Keith's attendance represented a very different stake in the experience. He was at Chartridge to find out about the partner organisation with whom he would be working closely over the next two years. If he was to co-ordinate the whole project he really needed to know about Youth at Risk and their methodology

Keith says that when, during the first session later that evening, he learned who his fellow participants were (it is Youth at Risk's practice to begin all their courses by asking participants to introduce and say something about themselves) he was seriously intimidated. In addition to myself as the Chair of the Youth Justice Board there was someone from the Cabinet Office, an administrator from a major

charity, the chief executive of a FTSE 100 company, and so on, about twenty of us in all. He wondered what on earth he was getting into.

Keith describes himself as always having had a bit of a chip on his shoulder: a Yorkshire lad bullied at school, he failed his music A Level, went to a poly rather than a university and thereafter, working in the arts field of the public sector, had always had to struggle to get funding for whatever he was doing. The result is that if he finds himself in an uncomfortable environment, he says he tends to react

defensively. He didn't feel at home at Chartridge. He thought he'd gone to the event with an open mind, but soon realised he hadn't. So within five minutes of the first training session starting Keith recalls that he began arguing with the trainer. The first exercise opened with the trainer asking his audience what they understood by the word distinction. Keith offered 'The top of the tree – the best'. Keith recalls the trainer rejecting his definition as wrong, which he felt was inappropriate. The trainer, he felt, should arguably have said 'Yes, that's one

meaning, one interpretation, but I'm looking for another meaning.'

I must have witnessed this exchange at Chartridge, whatever it was that happened, but I have no recollection of it. I can only vaguely recall thinking Keith the sort of person to be among the first to put up his hand in a group. But for Keith this was a déjà vu moment clearly imprinted on his brain. Although he didn't think that Mark, the trainer, handled his defensive behaviour well, Keith says that at this point he thought to himself: 'I'm being defensive. If I'm going to get something out of this course, I've got to change my attitude.' Thereafter he tried to learn and concentrate. He admits he struggled and that for about fifty per cent of the time he had no idea what the trainer was on about and wondered whether everyone else was in the same boat. But early in the afternoon on the second day he says a penny dropped. He could suddenly see what they were getting at. He didn't get it all and says that he still doesn't get it all. Throughout the next two years he has continued to discuss with the Youth at

Risk trainers how they attempt to get their message across. Keith estimates he has subsequently been to at least 15 YAR-led groups and that he got something further out of every one, and not just because he'd forgotten some of the elements. But at Chartridge he got the core of it. Indeed he says he doesn't remember the drive back home from Chartridge to the Black Country: his head being in such a whirl trying to make sense of what he'd learned.

Critical to Keith for the penny to drop was the importance of commitment: of honouring undertakings given to others in order that trust be built, of turning up for meetings at the time you've said you'll turn up, of doing precisely what you've told the kids you're going to do. He says he accepted that hitherto he hadn't always done that in his professional life and how it had now been dinned into him that if youth workers didn't do that, how could they reasonably expect the kids to do it?

Back in Dudley Keith's immediate task was to support Andrew Sparke finalise the contract documentation with the other local authorities. In doing so, two aspects of the provisional project plan preoccupied him. First, his title and, secondly, YAR's suggested timetable.

Getting the Show on the Road

Keith says he's not much for titles, but knows that they are nonetheless significant. He thought that if he was going to have to deal with local authority chief executives and departmental heads in all the agencies involved, people generally called directors or managers, then his suggested title, co-ordinator, wouldn't cut the mustard. It wouldn't enable him to get the access or attention he would need. He wouldn't have the necessary status. He therefore argued, successfully, that his title be changed to Project Director. His second tier project colleagues, within the local authorities, would be called project co-ordinators.

This change to Keith's title was not liked by everyone: it implied that Keith was authorised to direct all aspects of the project. The Artistic and Education Directors at Birmingham Royal Ballet, for example, were adamant that Keith was not qualified to direct the dance aspect of the project and should not interfere with artistic issues. Keith was required to give his assurance that dance direction would be the exclusive province of Birmingham Royal Ballet.

Keith's title was also to give rise to tensions with Birmingham City Council, whose senior officers appeared to feel that the servant of a smaller local authority, Dudley, should not be directing a project to which they, one of the largest local authorities in the land, were contributing half the funds. They and key people at Birmingham Royal Ballet had always felt that someone from Birmingham should be directing the project and whether for personal or status reasons, Keith's position as Project Director was periodically undermined.

It was entirely understandable that Keith felt vulnerable with his title during his first weeks in the job. At this stage he had no office, no staff and no administrative support, though he did have a lap-top – an old one inherited from his former job – and a mobile phone - his own. He was starting from scratch with no one with the practical experience to tell him how to do what he had to do. Further, when he looked at Youth at Risk's timetable for the project it was clear to him that it could not be delivered and had to be changed. Indeed the tight timetable was relaxed, an outcome which, interestingly, Neil Wragg accepts had to happen. There is an aspect of YAR's philosophy at issue here which needs to be understood.

YAR sees itself as a change agent. As such the organisation operates on the premise of impossible or unreasonable deadlines. It's a YAR technique.

Neil argues that complex change programmes can't succeed on the basis of decision by committee which can lead to endless prevarication and delay. So, he argues, when YAR steps into a local authority arena YAR is the change agent because at that stage no one in the local authority owns whatever programme is contemplated. YAR has to say: 'This is what we can do for you. Give us permission... [and, then] This is what we're going to do. This is the date when it's going to start. These are the arrangements.'

They maintain that if they don't say that, if they don't set immediate deadlines and stipulate demanding resource allocations, things don't happen. Without a seriously challenging impetus people who are scared or don't want change make sure that change doesn't happen, the initiative dies, strangled by bureaucracy. So, when a green light has been shown locally from above and people lower down the managerial chain say 'We can't do that', YAR's tendency is to respond 'Yes you can' and insist on holding people to a very tight schedule. However, once they feel that all parties have taken ownership of the initiative and are indicating that they want it to happen, then YAR is prepared to let the timetable slip because they know that the dates originally set are if not impossible, then certainly unreasonable.

It follows that Keith's contention that the dates first set by YAR for the recruitment of people who the contract with the local authorities called trailblazers and life coaches were operationally not feasible, was soon accepted by YAR.

Stocktake

Keith had decided that YAR's methodology had a lot to offer. As early as October 2004 four local authorities had verbally agreed to participate in the project (though the contract was not actually signed until 14 January 2005) and all four authorities were taking steps to appoint staff to run the project. Local ownership had been secured. The timetable was therefore relaxed and, in Keith's eyes, made deliverable.

Finally Keith decided that Ballet Who? was not a good title under which to recruit young people of the sort the project was aimed at. So, following a suggestion from someone at BRB, the project's working title became Leaps & Bounds. Indeed it was only in the months immediately prior to the Hippodrome performance in September 2006 that the original title, slightly modified – Ballet Hoo! – was resuscitated for both the show and the subsequent television series.

A's Story

A lives in a smallish semi-detached house on a large council estate in Kings Norton, which, despite its ancient origins, is today a predominantly white working class, sprawling suburb about five miles from the centre of Birmingham on the southern side of the city. The houses in the part of the estate where A. lives look well kept and outside each of the garages in her cul de sac are smart, newish cars. The inside of the house is equally smart with new furniture and fittings.

I met A's Mum and two of her brothers,

one of her brother's partners and their small baby. I sat in the front room talking to A while everyone else congregated in the kitchen in the back of the house.

I'm 17 and I live with my Mum. My parents came from Jamaica, but I haven't been there. My Mum and Dad split up a long time ago. I'm currently at the Cadbury College 6th Form College in Kings Norton. Before that I went to Kings Norton Girls School where I got 10 GCSE passes, 9 Cs and an A in Art.

I want to be a fashion photographer.

I got into the Leaps & Bounds project largely by chance. A friend at school had heard about it and suggested I come along with her. I was told it involved dance and was going to be on TV. Since I had always taken part in school shows and had been in a dance group from the age of 13, I thought it sounded good. When I was interviewed and asked what my three principal life goals were I said: controlling my temper; becoming a better dancer; and becoming more fit and healthy.

When the TV documentary talked about the young people involved being disadvantaged, I didn't think it applied to me personally. I didn't think I was disadvantaged. But I recognised that I came from a generally disadvantaged area and that I didn't go to a good school. My school came 80th out of 80 schools in Birmingham when it came to exam results, so by that standard it was the worst. And the 6th form college I go to now doesn't have very good results either. But I didn't personally like being called disadvantaged and I was embarrassed when the

TV series was shown. This was partly because I had told everyone to watch it and in the end – though I was filmed quite a lot - I wasn't in it. But it was also because of the way we were shown. My Mum wasn't pleased. Friends rang her and said how could you put your child in that bad children show – it's like Brat Camp. That aspect didn't bother me.

I would have liked to have figured more prominently in the TV series. But I understand why I didn't. I didn't have a big part in the final production and I wasn't involved in anything dramatic. I didn't lose my temper or anything like that, indeed the project helped me learn how not to. I get aggro, but I think I handle it better now. I did have problems at secondary school. I got into lots of fights and was suspended loads of times when I was about 12, 13 and 14. Once I was sent to a sort of pupil referral unit for two weeks and I was excluded from my school for good just before I was due to take my GCSEs. But I got them anyway.

I was picked on by other kids. Race may have had something to do with it. This is a white area so in my school there were only about six to eight non-white kids in each year of over a hundred kids – probably two black, three or four mixed race and three or four Asian. Also the teachers didn't understand. When we went swimming, for example, they were always telling me to hurry up. They didn't understand how I had to put cream on my skin. I think I would have done better had I gone to a more mixed school in a multi-cultural area.

I don't think my Mum thought I was a particular problem. She was used to it. So she wasn't phased. I'm

one of four in the family and my three older brothers all got into trouble. They've all been to prison. One is in prison now.

Four students from my school started on the Leaps & Bounds project but the other three dropped out after the four-day intensive. They couldn't handle it and left. I found it difficult. They had this 'conversation cup' which was held when someone was asked to talk about themselves. Every time that happened I jumped out of my chair and went to the toilet. I could never just sit there and handle it. But towards the end I started to listen and it did help me. I eventually talked about myself, like getting into fights

and that. When the other students from my school dropped out of the project I wanted to as well. Denzil (The Project Co-ordinator for Birmingham) persuaded me to stay and I'm glad I did.

The performances during the Leaps & Bounds project were amazing. We did a show at the Drum Theatre in Aston in March 2006. It was fantastic. I had performed on a stage bigger than that and with more audience before – but it still felt like a different experience, and I liked it. I had some doubts about doing Phase 2 of the project because I didn't want to fall behind at college. But I thought: I've come this far, I can't give up now. In the final performance at the Hippodrome I played a harlot and I loved the role. I got to flirt and dance with the boys. My Mum and her best friend and my brothers came. That evening was amazing. Straight afterwards my eyes started streaming with tears. Even though I had performed at the Hippodrome before I loved every minute of being on stage and I didn't want to come off.

My father died of cancer shortly after the performance. I didn't find it upsetting. He'd had cancer for years and we'd joked about what he was going to leave me.

I've continued dancing, but then I was doing that before Leaps & Bounds so I'm not sure that I learnt that much from that side of the project. I've been in a dance group since I was 13. I'm currently in a group called CRC. There are about 18-20 of us. It's an almost entirely black group. We do hip hop contemporary dance. And we do shows. I'm doing one this week.

I want to go to university to do photography. I've just had the results of my A/S levels. I got an A in Drama and a D in Photography, which is very disappointing. I broke a school camera during the year and had to make do with a camera from home which isn't very good. I'll have to do better next year.

I would have gone on to college without Leaps & Bounds.

But the project did help me. And through it I got to know a big social network. If they do projects like that again it should be a bit different. The four-day intensive shouldn't be so intensive and it shouldn't all come at the beginning. Bits of it should come later.

Before leaving A's house I chatted to her Mum and brothers in the kitchen. All very friendly. They gave me directions for my next appointment.

chapter 3

'damn contracts'

Combining art with personal development training

The unique aspect of the Ballet Hoo! project was the use of personal development training alongside the pursuit of artistic excellence. YAR believes that artistic learning and achievement is less likely to happen if personal problems and feelings of the young people are not adequately exposed and addressed.

That is to say YAR has an "integrated approach" to arts related education.

This method varies considerably from most arts based education projects which do not include personal development training and rely exclusively on participation in the artistic activity to produce results. A good illustration of this approach is that taken by the Birmingham Repertory Company.

The Birmingham Repertory Company was initially prepared to contribute to the Ballet Hoo Project. Stephen Ball, the Rep's Director of Education was invited to the early meetings and the idea was that the Rep, a highly prestigious theatre company which does a great deal of work with young people in the West Midlands, should lay on theatre workshops as part of the early, personal development training. The invitation was logical. The roles some of the young people went on to perform in Romeo and Juliet were as much theatrical expression as dance. Birmingham Rep provides programmes aiming to give young people opportunities to, 'gain confidence and self-esteem… a sense of achievement through performance and rehearsal process…be part of a team…gain a sense of belonging…creatively explore [their] own ideas…and promote the work of young people and issues that are relevant to young people through performance and workshops'.

Stephen Ball attended a YAR presentation in early 2005 and Julia Rainsford, one of the Rep's education officers subsequently delivered a series of theatre workshops during Phase One of the project. However, neither Stephen or Julia underwent YAR's training (something she says she subsequently regretted because it meant she failed fully to understand where the young people were coming from) and Steve subsequently declined to get the Birmingham Rep involved in Leaps & Bounds follow-on projects. Why?

The Birmingham Rep model is firstly that young people learn through theatre: by doing it. They learn through the text of whatever theatrical piece they are performing (the human emotions and relationships articulated by the text) and they learn through the practice of using the text (teamwork, discipline, and the like). They may thereby learn how better to deal with whatever personal issues are troubling their own lives but they are not expected to reveal those personal issues within the theatrical workshop: nor should they. Drama teachers are not social workers or therapists and thus the two spheres are separate: personal problems and issues are to the greatest possible extent left at the door. That is, the young people learn through fiction, occupying a safe space in which they can explore issues. The safe space is real, but at the same time not real. That, for Stephen Ball, is the essence of arts education. It is a model which Michelle Bould, the project coordinator for Sandwell described as a 'one step removed' approach.

Secondly Stephen believes it is not a good idea to have a concentration of disaffected or problematic young people together and the young people who take part in the Rep's theatrical workshops are diverse, mixed groups who have the opportunity to learn from each other.

For Stephen Ball the theatrical experience is the thing, whereas for YAR, he suggests, the artistic activity, be it contemporary dance, ballet, theatre, music, is a mere adjunct to the YAR personal development training. The parallel activity could just as well be a sport, or gardening, or rock climbing. It doesn't matter. The activity is merely a metaphor, a catalyst, through which the lessons learned in the personal development training can be put into practice.

Herein lies some truth, though not the whole truth; in some circumstances the possible parallel activities are interchangeable. The Ballet Hoo project might, for example, have been a pure theatre project with the Birmingham Repertory Company, or a music project with the Birmingham Symphony Orchestra. In that sense the parallel activity is not put on a pedestal; is not regarded as an irreplaceable essence. Yet it is important to understand that YAR's view is not demeaning to the activity, nor does it mean that the parallel activity can be any activity. On the contrary. First, the activity must be the embodiment of excellence and its practitioners must exhibit mastery. Secondly, the activity must provide an appropriate foil to the character of the group being trained.

Neil Wragg, YAR's Chief Executive explains this approach as follows. Many of the young people with whom his organisation works live in environments of hopelessness and second-rateness. Many have repeatedly been let down by most adults with whom they've had contact. Many of them have also been told so often that they're useless, no good at anything, failures, no-hopers or bad, that they've internalised those messages to the point where it has become their self identity; they believe it to be true of themselves. At the core of YAR's approach is the proposition that it's vital to break through the full-on, negative, iPod messages that are blasting away in the heads of young people if an impact is to be made, if learning is to become possible, and fresh life-changing choices achieved. There are several ingredients to this. First, is the language employed in the personal development training. Second, is the example of the teachers, the role models, who train the young people in whatever skill they are inducted alongside the personal development training. This is vital because, frankly, many of the young people's previous mentors, supervisors, advisors or teachers have been less than excellent role models, either because they're not very good at what they do or, to make life easier for themselves, they collude with the negative behaviour of the young people.

They've learned to live with young people's low expectations and they're often ground down themselves.

As will be seen in the final chapter, the Leaps & Bounds team have adapted the 'integrated approach' for its follow on projects. They do not reject the 'one step removed' approach to arts education, indeed Michelle Bould and Keith Horsfall have hitherto spent most of their working careers engaged in it. They accept the idea, that, with reference to dance education, for example, individuals have multiple intelligences and that kinesthenic learning, the development of muscle memory, has beneficial spillover consequences for the development of other intelligences and the acquisition of other skills.

Nor do they question art or drama therapy – a separate, professional field in its own right. What they do argue is that there are thousands of young people out there in the community leading deeply troubled lives and confronting serious personal problems, who will never get near a therapist or support worker of any sort. They're not even on the waiting lists. They're under the radar. Then there are others who might get a brief, strictly rationed dose of such services but who, after a few weeks or months, will be removed from whatever programme they're on.

They argue that if one simply takes such young people and place them in some sort of artistic training, in most cases, it won't work. Personal development training needs to be part of an integrated package. They are convinced YAR's approach enables the young people to grapple with and break free from their personal burden – liberates them to such an extent that, through the accompanying artistic endeavour, they can make genuine choices and express themselves more fully.

Irrespective of whether one agrees with the inclusion of personal development training in arts education, a number of people, including Stephen Ball disagree with the actual approach taken by YAR at its personal development training sessions.

Stephen Ball had a number of serious reservations. The presentation he attended was led by an American YAR trainer, who, following his questioning aspects of what she outlined, he overheard commenting that 'they [meaning Stephen Ball and possibly others] hadn't been processed properly'. He admits this alerted anti-American prejudices in him. He thought the remark insultingly patronising. It suggested to him that YAR had a mechanical approach to issues and young people, although neither he or Julia Rainsford actually attended or observed a training session. Nevertheless they felt, on the basis of what they had heard, that YAR's insistence on certain rules being followed was authoritarian and incompatible with showing respect to young people. It was for this reason that after discussion with Stephen, Julia withdrew from providing theatre workshops to the project. She was particularly upset by a YAR decision to exclude one youth from the project for refusing to remove his baseball cap during a training session. She considered that decision disproportionate, and the REP's withdrawal reflected a lack of sympathy with what they took to be YAR's philosophy. In fact, as the Leaps & Bounds team are at pains to emphasise, no young person ever gets thrown off their projects. The young people agree to abide by ground rules, their parents agree that their offspring should follow the ground rules, and if they breach the ground rules they are made to confront the fact and asked to honour their commitments. At this point they may decide to take themselves off the project, but if they do so, that is their decision, not the project team's.

Stephen also had reservations about the involvement of Diverse Productions and the TV cameras. He thought it was going to lead to a lot of acting up. He recalls that Diverse had initially wanted to have a 'diary room' on Big

Brother lines. He considered it dangerous for young people to expose themselves before large numbers of other young people and in front of the cameras, with possible exposure on TV. Finally, he did not like the proposition that the project would be for young people who were all in some way disadvantaged. It would not be the sort of diverse group he favoured.

It appears then that YAR's personal development training sessions can excite the animosity of some participants and observers who either walk out in high dudgeon or fail to reappear after the first session or day.

The Ground Rules

This was true during the Ballet Hoo! sessions for trailblazers, life coaches and young people. The trigger is often the detailed explanation of the ground rules or their early enforcement. When the young people enrolled they were all asked to sign a contract agreeing to abide by the ground rules though, as several subsequently pointed out, signing a piece of paper is one thing, appreciating the words that are written on the paper is another. The ground rules were:

- to stay at all course sessions and/or project activities until I am told there is a break and not leave the project venue, run away or hide;
- to be on time at all sessions and follow all instructions given to me;
- not to eat anything during a course session unless instructed, not use drugs or intoxicants during the course session or activities;
- to smoke only in designated smoking areas and only during designated smoking breaks;
- to inform my project co-ordinator of medications my doctor told me to take;
- to wear my name tag at course sessions and project activities and not write on, mark, or put graffiti on it;
- not to provoke, bother, irritate or tease people at any time during the personal development training and follow-through programme;

- not fight, hit or engage in violence;
- not to take anything that does not belong to me and not deface or destroy property at the venue;
- if upset and/or frustrated during my participation I agree to communicate responsibly to my project co-ordinator or other member of staff or volunteer;
- to participate 100% in the Leaps & Bounds programme; this includes sharing myself;
- to support all the other participants in keeping their agreements.
- on arrival at personal development group sessions, to fill up seats from the front and centre as you arrive – that is, don't go for seats at the back;
- to remove hats
- to switch off mobile phones, ipods, etc.

Practically every category of participant can recall colleagues conspicuously refusing to accept one or other of these rules, be it a life coach shouting "I'm not going to be spoken to like that" when rebuked for arriving late and being required to discuss whether they had really committed themselves to arriving on time, a social worker trailblazer refusing to wear a name badge, or Afro-Caribbean youths or youth workers angrily refusing to take off hats they considered part of their identity. Making an issue out of what the critics saw as trivia or unreasonable demands was said to reflect the authoritarian, arrogant, patronising, disrespectful or disproportionate preoccupations of the

trainers. It was also the source of a 'bullying' accusation.

By contrast YAR argues that clear ground rules are vital to their method. Namely, to instil an appreciation that all effective human interaction relies on a mutually understood and followed code of behaviour of some sort and commitments to others have to be honoured if respect is to be earned. In that sense it is not a particular, substantive ground rule that is being made an issue, but the concept of following ground rules in general that is important – though, self-evidently the YAR ground rules are carefully chosen and are important in their own right. In the case of the targeted young people –

those disadvantaged or 'at risk', who often come from anarchic situations in which there is a chronic absence of discipline, structure and routine – the concept of ground rules is crucial. Being prepared to follow ground rules is the springboard for whatever other activity is attached to the personal development training, that is, through personal discipline and showing respect for others, social teams can be built, excellence achieved and joyful activity engaged in that spells personal fulfilment. The sum of the group can, to every individual's benefit, be far greater than the sum of the separate, constituent parts. As we shall see, even those young people who were critical of aspects of their initial personal development

training, learned these lessons. Further, the Leaps & Bounds team, now organising further arts projects for young people are adamant that firm adherence to ground rules is a vital ingredient for success.

When introducing their programmes to potential clients YAR's approach is explained in the following terms:

YAR's Personal Development Programme

"We work with groups of people who, through what they experience during our training, discover who they might be. They find out that, despite what they may have thought about themselves or others, they are valuable and have a future. They see for themselves that they do not have to have a predictable life of unfulfilled potential. They have a choice. They don't have to stick with the past. There is a way out.

This voyage of discovery is run by a highly trained course leader who is supported by a team of totally committed people who include child protection experts and

psychotherapists. We explore, with each individual, their own beliefs. This allows them to see other opportunities and options and understand which of their beliefs are best suited to their achieving what they really want. The process can be both challenging and intense."

The sessions take the form of guided group conversations in which the young people examine and share significant events, core beliefs, decisions, values, problems, issues and concerns. They examine the costs and benefits of past choices and behaviour. They share past resentments and regrets. They look at their relationships with friends, family and authority figures. They examine their past and current actions and discover whether they are getting what they say they want out of life. Through these discussions, they get to the source of their behaviours and actions and why their lives may not be working.

The aim is to create a lasting change in the mind-set which will, in turn, lead participants to alter their actions and behaviours, thereby enabling them to fulfil more of their potential. Participants ideally become more able to create and sustain effective working relationships, see how to create goals for themselves, remain focussed on those goals even when faced with difficult circumstances, and discover how they can take full responsibility for who they are and what they do.

For the process to work it is crucial that those who participate:

- choose actively to get involved;
- pin-point and identify goals which realistically reflect the way they would like their future to be;
- commit themselves to do everything it takes to reach the goals they have chosen;
- let YAR staff become involved in steering them

towards a positive end result;
- identify the people in their lives who may not be committed to their achieving their goals;
- come to understand how the way they see their past experiences may have impacted negatively on the choices they have made;
- appreciate there may be a difference between the facts of any given situation and their interpretation of them;
- determine what behaviour will best help them attain the goals they have set themselves;
- understand and welcome the support of everybody who is willing them to succeed;
- practice what they have learnt.

None of this is easy. The process is emotionally demanding. Difficult decisions have to be made. Honesty and openness are the keys to success.

Life Coaches

Personal development life coaching is a fundamental plank in YAR's approach because much of what the YAR training seeks to instill is not understood immediately. It is difficult. The young people require additional individualised support. The contract between YAR and the local authorities defined the life coach role as follows:

'One to one support for the young people throughout the programme. Their main task is to coach and support the young people in achieving their goals and participating in the follow through sessions.'

Life coaches were to be recruited by the commercial recruitment agency Alexander Mann & Co with which YAR had previously worked (one of their directors is an avid supporter of YAR and regularly assists it as part of her firm's corporate responsibility commitment). Once recruited the life coaches were to be trained and supported by YAR.

However, for various unforeseen reasons the agency failed to recruit the number of volunteer life coaches required and the volunteers who were recruited were not found early enough for all the young people to be allocated a life coach when they were enrolled in spring 2005.

Everyone agrees that this aspect of the Ballet Hoo project did not work as intended and, as we shall see, the Dudley-based continuation project, Leaps & Bounds, has decided that next time round things will be done differently.

There are differing views about what sort of people should, ideally, undertake the role of life coach. The Leaps & Bounds project team think they should be local people with whom the youth can easily identify. YAR considers that coaches should ideally be persons relatively distant from the neighbourhoods and culture the young people inhabit. These two models for mentoring or life coaching we might characterise as comfort as opposed to challenge, though most schemes comprise elements of both: it's usually a question of degree as to which model is emphasised and the mix of persons recruited. The differences nevertheless needs spelling out because they relate to YAR's philosophy more generally.

Why was Neil Wragg keen that a commercial recruitment agency,

relatively distant from the Ballet Hoo project (albeit the firm has an office in the West Midlands as well as in London), recruit the life coaches whereas the Dudley-based Leaps & Bounds team think, both then and today, that life coach volunteers are best recruited by them locally? Neil explains the issue as follows:

"We want the young people to engage with and be coached by people who are very different from themselves. People who are successfully employed, who are progressing in their careers and who are the embodiment of all the discipline that entails. Many of them will ideally be employed in commercial companies. We want that because we think the young people should be exposed to values and attitudes different to those likely to

prevail in their immediate neighbourhoods. We think that if they are so exposed they will possibly have less of a rude awakening when they go out to get a job and we think they should be made aware that less permissive attitudes to much youth behaviour operates in the commercially successful world. In summary, we think that life coaches should ideally be far off from the world that is familiar to the young people and, because it's not easy to recruit such volunteers, we think the task will most likely be done successfully by a commercial recruitment company with those sorts of contacts."

This, on the surface, is a different approach from that used by many mentoring schemes. Several organisations working in the youth justice field, The Youth Advocates Programme in

London for example, argue that mentors should ideally come from the same ethnic groups and neighbourhoods from which the young people are drawn and that there is an advantage in the volunteers having had similar experiences to the young people they're working with. Such volunteers, they argue, are more likely to be credible to the young people and will prove more comfortable for them to relate to. The volunteers will more readily appreciate what the young people are experiencing. Further, such volunteers will most easily be recruited through the networks which the youth service is likely to have locally and, because the volunteers are more likely to live locally, the arrangements will also work better practically. That is, put bluntly, the volunteers are more likely to be on hand when they are needed: they'll probably turn up.

Neil Wragg has no problem with the proposition that life coaches should ideally replicate the ethnic composition of the young people being coached. On the contrary, he thinks that ideal. He also thinks it excellent if coaches have had experiences in their youth similar to those that the young people are facing. But for him it is important that coaches have overcome and grown away from those experiences, that they've risen above them. For otherwise coaches sharing the same cultural backgrounds and experiences as the young people may reinforce precisely that which needs challenging. Moreover, he argues that local authority teams tend to recruit volunteers from the local authority networks with which they are familiar – people from the estates, employed in the public

services, enjoying job security, operating within a tradition of public service and having a tendency to hold permissive assumptions and attitudes. That is, they are unlikely to be representative of the tougher labour market which the young people will be likely to be exposed to in the future. He thinks that life coaching has to be both challenging and rigorous and doubts that this more professional approach will be delivered by using the traditional local authority networks.

In the event the recruitment difficulty encountered during the Ballet Hoo! project meant that the local authorities primarily engaged local people as life coaches.

The Contract

Under the direction of Andrew Sparke, Dudley council had become the lead authority for the project. He had the enthusiastic backing of his elected Council Leader and being a lawyer he worked with Ben Rose, YAR's London-based co-founder, trustee and legal adviser, to draw up a contract. Andrew understood the risks the project entailed and realised this new way of working between youth and arts services would require a dedicated team with adequate staffing and financial resources.

The deal that was struck to take the project forward was complex, covering the financing, management and staffing of a project which was to run for 18 months for up to 300 young people.

There were two, quite separate financial packages for the Ballet Hoo! Project: that between YAR and the local authorities, Black Country Connexions Ltd and the Learning and Skills Council, the principal funders, and that between YAR and BRB, Diverse Productions and Channel 4.

YAR was to receive £300,000 over two years for training services, throughout the project. Birmingham City Council agreed to pay £150,000 and Dudley council Sandwell M.B.C., Wolverhampton City Council, Black Country Connexions Ltd and the Black Country Learning and Skills Council were to pay £30,000 each, over a two year period.

YAR also agreed to contract with BRB to secure those elements of coaching required from BRB in the personal development training programme and for the production of the Ballet "Romeo and Juliet", and also with Channel 4 television for the filming of the training programme and the ballet to be screened on national television.

YAR

YAR's role was to:

- Create an enrolment process that was thorough and prepared the young people for the project and specifically for the personal development work.
- Support the local authorities in the recruitment and enrolment of the young people through youth professionals (the co ordinators and trailblazers).

- Recruitment of life coaches with the help of Alexander Mann and Co.
- Deliver a series of four day initial intensive personal development training for the young people giving them the opportunity to "examine" their current reality and create a new stand for their future.
- Train staff who were to be involved in the project in YAR's methodology.

- Assist the local authorities in the delivery of follow-through sessions for the young people to allow the group to re-connect to the four day training and make stronger links between the other work they were doing and their life goals
- Provide regular follow-through sessions for youth co-ordinators, life coaches and trailblazers.

The Local Authorities

The Leaps & Bounds project office, headed by the Project Director Keith Horsfall, was established to deliver this large and complex project. It had managerial responsibility for the project co-ordinators, life coaches, trailblazers, the programme activities (including travel, venues and hospitality), as well as overall responsibility for the young people (including any child protection issues) and for liaison with partners.

The contract stipulated that there should be two project co-ordinators (originally termed 'managers' in the contract documentation), one for the three Black Country local authorities and the other for Birmingham. However, it was apparent almost from the outset that having a single co-ordinator for the three Black Country authorities wouldn't work. The incumbent wouldn't have the required knowledge and network outside the local authorities from which they were recruited. So it was agreed that each of the four local authorities should appoint a co-ordinator from within their authority.

The local authorities had the task of 'using their best endeavours' to enrol the 300 young people onto the project in accordance with YAR's Enrolment Policy.

In addition the local authorities were required to provide no fewer than 80 youth professionals (40 in Birmingham, 12 each in Dudley, Sandwell and Wolverhampton, Black Country Connexions providing the remaining four) to undertake the role of trailblazer. This included identifying and referring young people who met the selection criteria to the programme, supporting them with the enrolment process, and thereafter keeping the young people in touch with the programme and supporting communication with their families.

The local authorities were also to support YAR in enrolling the appropriate number of volunteers to act as life coaches for the young people whose role would be to support their assigned young person throughout the programme and help them achieve their life goals.

In conjunction with YAR the local authorities were also responsible for the organisation and delivery of the 'follow-through' elements of the programme. Black Country Connexions

Black Country Connnexions was not simply a funder contributing to YAR's fees.

BCC also delivered:

- The establishment and ongoing support of a project office
- Referral of young people to the project
- The secondment of three personal advisers (PA's) with expertise in dealing with disadvantaged and 'at risk' young people on the project, one for each of the participating Black Country councils.

Birmingham Royal Ballet

BRB wanted to extend their education and artistic work to young people who would not normally access their programmes. They also wanted to explore the contribution of ballet to the lives of young people through performance. They were interested in broadening their audience and making ballet more accessible and saw the television programme as a great opportunity to reach new audiences and promote BRB and Birmingham.

BRB was responsible for the artistic elements of the project. Desmond Kelly, Assistant Artistic Director of BRB, became the artistic director of the Ballet Hoo! Company, assisted by Marion Tait, BRB's Ballet Mistress, and other dancers from the Company. The team was to support and train the young people throughout the project, culminating in the performance of Romeo and Juliet.

BRB's Education Director was to lead on the co-ordination of the project for BRB which included its press and PR, technical and wardrobe departments as well as a large artistic team of dancers and free-lance artists.

Diverse Productions

Diverse Productions was commissioned by Channel 4 to follow the project from the beginning with the purpose of making three, one hour television programmes and one of ninety minutes tracking the journey of the young people and highlighting how the partners worked together. The last ninety minute programme would show excerpts of the performance. Contracts were drawn up with the young people to gain their permission for the use of material throughout the project. A contract was also drawn up with BRB for additional rehearsals with their dancers and the BRB Sinfonia in order to accommodate the final week's preparations and performance. A dedicated team, led by Michael Waldman, series producer and director, Claire Lasko, producer and director of the programmes, and Karen Pearson, who took over from Farne Sinclair as associate producer, working with a regular sound and camera crew, were to take an active interest in the planning and management of the project throughout.

Other Contributors

The Arts Council England funded the educational costs connected with the filming and the evaluation report.

Virgin trains supported the travel costs of the project for staff and life coaches.

Sandwell College provided BTEC accreditation.

Aston Villa Football Club delivered fitness sessions during the summer.

The Programme

January to September 2005
(Phase 1, Part 1)

- 'Kick off' workshop for stakeholders – meeting for key players and future friends of the project to support the design.
- Training for local authority and BRB staff likely to be involved with the project.
- Specific training for project co ordinators, trailblazers and life coaches.
- The recruitment and enrolment of the young people across the four local authorities.

- Four-day intensive personal development sessions for the young people and the staff and volunteer life coaches supporting them.

From September 2005 – March 2006 (Phase 1 Part 2) Follow-through training and events: a series of training sessions and events to give the young people the opportunity to address the life goals they had set themselves in the initial training, practice a healthier life style and be more engaged with the opportunities available to them in their communities.

April – September 2006
(Phase 2):

The Ballet – the young people working as one company Ballet Hoo!

- Company formation evening for the young people who wanted to continue with the project and be involved in the ballet.
- Programme of artistic training by BRB staff in preparation for the performance of Romeo and Juliet in September.
- Personal development workshops to run alongside the ballet training.

It was never intended that all the young people would go on to do the ballet. Indeed an early briefing by BRB estimated a figure of 70 participants for Phase 2. It was however, always anticipated that at whatever point a young person left the project something would have changed for the better in their lives.

The Management Structure

There were two levels of management: a Steering Group comprising senior representatives from the various partners and an operational structure that managed the project to its final conclusion.

The operational structure comprised various groups which were set up to support the organisation of the project and report to the Partners

Steering Group:

- Project Management Group involving the Project Director, the project co ordinators, Birmingham Royal Ballet, Youth at Risk, Diverse Productions, Black Country Connexions.
- Follow-through group – similar to the above group but involving those who had recently delivered workshops. They would meet to review the work, identify particular issues and decide next steps.

- Meeting of Project Director/project co-ordinators/Youth at Risk to plan the inputs with the young people and life coaches.
- Press and public relations group made up of staff from BRB, the local authorities, Diverse Productions and YAR.
- A Youth Forum comprising two elected young people from each local authority, the Project Director and pastoral staff.

S's Story

S together with her grandfather, lives in a small, semi-detached, three bedroom council house, in a cul-de-sac, on a large council estate in Yardley, three miles east of the centre of Birmingham. The postage stamp-sized front and back gardens are overgrown with grass. The bathroom and toilet are downstairs, off the kitchen. The walls of the living room are adorned with several large, studio-taken, framed photographs of four black young people, grouped closely together, smiling broadly. The room is dominated by a large sofa on which S's grandfather spends the greater part of his time. He answers the front door, asking me through it who I am before he lets me in. I chat to him for a while before S comes down and after a decent interval S and I go into the back garden to talk. It's a warm summer morning under a clear blue sky.

I'm 16 and I've lived the whole of my life in Yardley, Birmingham. I live with my 74 year old grandfather. There are just the two of us. My two older sisters and brother used to live here as well. But they've left home now. They all live in the Birmingham area, but none close by. My Granddad is blind. He's been blind for three or four years. He had a stroke and he's a diabetic. A nurse comes in twice a day to give him his injections. Someone else visits every day with food to heat up, but it's not proper cooking. The local council is talking to Granddad about a care home. But I don't know when that's likely to happen.

Granddad is not my real granddad. He lived with my Nan, but they weren't married. When my Nan died my Granddad took us all on and looked after us. I've lived in this house with him ever since I was two. That was when my Dad killed my Mum.

I don't really know much about what happened to my Mum or what happened to my Dad as a result of his killing my Mum. My family never talk about it. My Granddad doesn't like to speak about those sorts of things and my sisters and brother don't seem to want to know. So I don't know whether my Dad was taken to court or sent to prison. I just know that I never had any contact with him until about three or four years ago. I would like a Dad, so I'd like to get to know him. I've met him three or four times, The last time I met him he was living in a rehab hostel – I don't know what sort of rehab - in Wolverhampton. I haven't seen him for a bit and I don't push it. I'll wait to see what happens. My Dad is about 40. He says he wants to have a relationship with me.

I owe so much to my Granddad and I feel sort of guilty about him. I'm out of the house a lot and very busy. So Granddad's left on his own for much of the time. He can't go out unless someone goes with him. It's a bit difficult. But I don't feel it as a great pressure. It's the life that I'm used to. I know my life isn't normal, but it's my life and I've coped with it. I haven't ever felt that my situation was particularly tough or that I was disadvantaged. And I've always been quite detached and felt sort of different to the rest of the family. There's a bit of an age gap between me and my sisters, and I've always felt slightly left out. There's not the same sisterly relationship between me and my sisters as there is between them. I admire my Granddad. He's devoted himself to us, and he wants the best for us. Yet he's not even a blood relative. I feel bad about him because I can't easily repay him for what he's done.

Race? It's not an issue in Yardley and it's never been a problem for me.

I was always the lowest of the low at home. But at school it was different. I was the big one. It's always been like that. Big for my age – much taller than other children - and in junior school I was always top of the class. So I was a big figure in every sense and very active. It's been like that right through school – singing and taking part in school theatrical productions. In secondary school I got into a bit of trouble. I often challenged teachers, so I wasn't popular with some of them. I've never liked being told to do something 'because I'm your teacher' or 'because I'm older than you'. I don't like that idea of levels of authority. I think respect has to be earned. So I suppose I've stood out at secondary school partly because I've pushed that line and some teachers have sometimes thought me rude. The consequence is that a lot of people know me. But they don't really know me, if you know what I mean, because

I keep myself pretty well to myself.

Race? It's not an issue in Yardley and it's never been a problem for me. My family came from Jamaica. I think my Granddad came in the 60s, but I don't know anything about the circumstances. I went to Jamaica in the summer of 2002 my first time abroad on an aeroplane, I'd like to go again. But I don't like discussions about 'black' and 'white'. I'd rather call it 'culture differentiation'.

I got into Leaps & Bounds almost by chance, because no one else in my school was involved and no one at my school knew about it. I'd never heard about it. My Granddad was worried about me at the time. I was only 14 and I was staying out late sometimes and he didn't know what I was doing. I don't think I was at risk of getting into trouble, but my Granddad thought I was and because he had lost his sight he couldn't do

much about it. He said I was getting into bad company and wasn't listening to him. He was worried about the "birds and the bees" occurring. I think he felt that because I didn't have a mother, there was no one to tell me about those things. So he called social services and they sent round a woman called a targeted family support worker. She talked to me a few times and researched various possibilities – my Granddad wanted me to be involved in something positive – and she came across the Leaps & Bounds project, I'm not entirely sure how. She arranged an interview for me. It was then that I met Denzil Peart [the Ballet Hoo! Co-ordinator for Birmingham]. I don't remember much about the interview. I just remember being quite reserved and feeling wary about what I was signing up for.

The four-day intensive experience at the beginning of Leaps & Bounds was for

me memorable for two things. There was a drama workshop which incorporated dance and movement. The woman who ran it told me before she left how she thought I was amazing and had something about me. I felt this could be a sign from the start, because I always think that things happen for a reason.

The other thing was that during one of the Youth at Risk group sessions I revealed that my Dad had killed my Mum when I was two. I told the group session run by Denise about it. I don't know what made me do it. I suppose I felt comfortable within the group about letting them know. But it became a big thing, because it was filmed. I discussed my concerns about having talked about it with Denzil and he reassured me that it would be OK. But it was decided that the film director, Michael, and Denzil should come and talk to my Granddad about it at home. I don't know what they said

because I wasn't there. But when I came home they were all together, my Granddad, my sisters, the film director and Denzil, and they were laughing and seemed relaxed. But of course this information about me and my Mum and Dad was in the TV series, and it was repeated more than once. I minded that. And though he didn't say anything Granddad got into a bit of a state when the TV series was shown and he heard it being said. He didn't like it. I don't think about it much now. I feel that it's out there, and that's that. But it did have some strange effects. I remember a girl coming up to me at school afterwards and saying that she'd cried when she saw

the TV series and learned that about me.

The TV series made me an even bigger figure at school. The staff and my friends were very supportive. I was very prominent in the TV film. I suppose that happened because the film director made a lot of what happened to my Mum, plus I had a big, dramatic part in the Hippodrome performance. I was pleased because I am ambitious. I wanted to be noticed. But there were downsides to all the attention. First, I was aware that the suggestion in the TV series that The Leaps & Bounds young people, myself included, were disadvantaged and that I was part of that crowd might

hurt me. It was another thing my Granddad didn't like. He says that the TV programme made us all out to be problem children, and that I'm not a problem child and he never thought I was. I also felt bad about the fact that I got so much attention and others did not. I am aware that some of the others may be jealous about it and think of me as acting superior. I don't want to feel or be seen to be superior. I just want to be mature about it.

I was also aware that I approached things differently on the night of the Hippodrome performance. I'm a person with sentimental values. So the performance had a deep

meaning for me. My part as Lady Capulet, Juliet's mother, required me to act grief. And I felt real empathy for the role, because it was ironic given my parenting circumstances. But, strangely, I wasn't that nervous on the night and I didn't cry. I don't show my emotions. I felt I should. But I didn't. When it was all over almost everyone cried. But once again I didn't.

I get my GCSE and BTec Performing Arts results tomorrow. I think it will be OK, though I'm bad at maths. I've applied for several 6th Form colleges, but I'll have to audition to do performing arts and I don't know whether I'll get in. I hope so because I really want success in the world of drama and TV (feature length films). I do everything I can to make progress to that end. I keep myself very busy because my aim is to get involved in as many things as I can. I was always in school productions. I play tuba in a wind band and got a Distinction at Grade 5 standard. I've taken part in the Yardley Festival. And this summer I've been a peer tutor for a University of the First Age Summer School. In previous years I've just been a student participant.

The Leaps & Bounds project and the Ballet Hoo series was a real opportunity for me. I wanted to see if, as a company, we could pull it off. I also wanted to see what was involved in a major production. From everything we were told it sounded as if the heat was going to be on, and I love pressure. I'm passionate about completing tasks and doing well in them. And by now my personal development was such that I was well interested and stuck in. I want success and I'm careful about not doing anything that might hinder opportunities for me. I

wouldn't tattoo myself, for example.

In the end I learnt a lot from the Leaps & Bounds project. And the experience made me want success even more. It's clear in my mind. I really want to be on TV in films.

I'm not religious. But I am sort of fatalistic. I really think that things have life outside my experience of them and that things happen for a reason. Where will I be in five years? I hope to be completing a performing arts degree and to have got even more experience. If I succeed in this, I'll be the first in my family. One of my sisters started a degree, but she left during her first year

when it became stressful.

I don't know how it will be if I don't get my dream.

S learned the day after I interviewed her that she got a Distinction in her Performing Arts Btec First Diploma, Bs in History and Music, Cs in English, Maths, English Literature, Media Studies and Home Economics and a double D in Combined Science double award. Following an audition she was accepted at the 6th Form College of her choice to do a Btec National Diploma in Performing Arts . She still lives with her Grandad in Yardley.

chapter 4

'filling the quotas'
Geography

The relationship between Birmingham and the Black Country, the historic industrial area which lies to the west of the city, parallels that within many other metropolitan areas in modern Britain: a city and a semi-urban hinterland whose resources gave it life and breadth.

Birmingham is Britain's third largest city and in terms of status has historically regarded itself as second to London with a population of approximately one million. It owes its growth, historical wealth and civic status to the manufacturing industry and this was built largely on the deposits of natural resources, coal and iron, that lay to the west, in the Black Country – an ill-defined area which is today taken to comprise Sandwell, Walsall, Wolverhampton and Dudley, four metropolitan councils, with a combined population larger than Birmingham.

In the Black Country lay outcropping coal seams among the thickest in Britain. From the medieval period onwards the villages of the Black Country combined agriculture with iron working and manufacture, smithying and nail making, subsequently chain and lock making, and many other trades. During the Industrial Revolution the Black Country was criss-crossed with a canal system linking it to the Severn to the west and Birmingham to the east. By the onset of the Victorian age it was one of the most heavily industrialised areas in Britain, black by day and red by night, the canal-side furnaces glowing in the dark and the pollution in the air matching the grime on the ground.

Neighbouring Birmingham – grandly claimed to have more miles of canals than Venice – became known as the first manufacturing town in the world. It was famous early on for making small arms. Birmingham was also home to major figures such as Matthew Boulton, James Watt and Joseph Priestley, who were at the forefront of the new technologies which in the 18th century underpinned the Industrial Revolution. It's population grew and Birmingham came to acquire all the modern public services and programmes; fire and police, slum clearance, piped water and sewerage, roads, street lighting, railways and electricity. It became a major, regional, administrative centre graced with fine civic amenities; a

splendid town hall, council house, law courts, museum and art gallery, parks and botanical gardens, giving it all the status of a grand city.

During the later 20th century the relationship between Birmingham and the Black Country changed. The Black Country became what is unkindly, but accurately, known as a rust-belt zone, losing much of its grime, but also much of its heart. By the 1960s coal mining had gone and though there remain small pockets of manufacturing there were far fewer working furnaces. The canals were cleaned up and restored to become a leisure resource. The signposts now point the way to Dudley's Black Country Living Museum where one can experience under ground

coal working or see demonstrations of metal working, sweet making or glass blowing.

These and other tourist attractions scarcely disguise an area of substantial economic deprivation and high unemployment. The roundabouts on the dual-carriageway arterial roads that dissect Dudley are today adorned with monumental metal castings which speak to the proud, creative, manufacturing heritage of the area. But there is little manufacturing work available nowadays and jobs are more often part-time and found in the supermarkets and consumer stores which stand by the arterial roads on the many brownfield sites that adorn the Black Country.

Meanwhile Birmingham, which during the 20th century became home to several major manufacturing plants, and was for that reason heavily bombed during the Second World War, also underwent major changes. In the '50s and '60s the centre of Birmingham was extensively and arguably brutally remodelled. New high-rise housing developments proliferated. But the manufacturing base of Birmingham, like that of the Black Country, declined and is today mostly reduced to small scale factories and tourist sites like the famous Jewellery Quarter. The Vickers Armstrong factory at Castle Bromwich has long since gone and the former MG-Rover plant at Longbridge stands as an iconic reminder of a manufacturing past almost certainly never to be resuscitated. Birmingham, like Britain generally, has become a centre for transportation and tourism, public and financial services, shopping and entertainment. Many of the high rise blocks from the post-War period have been demolished and a modern, impressive arts centre has been built in the heart of the city incorporating Birmingham's new Symphony Hall and Repertory Theatre close by the splendidly renovated Gas Street Canal Basin.

These physical transformations were accompanied by significant changes in the population of the city. After 1948 Birmingham became host to significant numbers of the Caribbean 'Windrush Generation'. This first, mass, minority ethnic migration, first from Jamaica and subsequently from elsewhere in the Caribbean, the Indian sub-continent and many other countries, may initially have been driven by short-term financial and educational betterment with a view to sending money back home and a return to countries of origin. But it did not turn out that way. Significant numbers of these immigrant groups made the West Midlands their permanent home, were joined by other members of their families and created identifiable communities with their own shops, community services and places of worship. Their children are Brummies or, if they live in the Black Country, Yamyams. The consequence is that Birmingham and parts of the Black Country have become among the most diverse communities in Britain. Thirty per cent of Birmingham's population today comprises non-white minority ethnic peoples, a higher proportion than London. One in seven of Birmingham's residents was born outside the United Kingdom. In the Black Country the picture is similar. In Wolverhampton and Sandwell 22 and 20 per cent of the population respectively comprises non-white ethnic minorities.

Birmingham's relative wealth, decline and recent transformation has always been accompanied by ecological divisions separating the affluent from the poor, the relatively advantaged from the relatively disadvantaged. These social class and cultural differences have in recent decades been consolidated with ethnic divides. Leafy Edgbaston ward, incorporating the University of Birmingham Campus, the Warwickshire Cricket Ground, the Botanical Gardens and a clutch of prestigious private schools, are literally a mile or two away from the wards of Lozells and East Handsworth within the district of Perry Barr.

Whereas the residents of the former are predominantly affluent, white and nominally Christian, 80% of the residents of the latter neighbourhoods are Muslims, mostly of Pakistani descent. Today the mosques, and temples of Birmingham and the Black Country are as prominent as the Christian churches and chapels and generally better attended.

It is also worth emphasising that the West Midlands is a cosmopolitan abstraction. That is not to say Birmingham, the Black Country and the neighbouring areas to the south, east and north lack any sense of common identity and purpose, but this is nonetheless a region with divided loyalties and strong, local, cultural identities. Both Birmingham and the Black Country incorporate territorial, cultural divisions which local residents understand all too well.

When Lambeth, London and many other inner city neighbourhoods erupted in race riots in spring 1981, so also did Handsworth, Birmingham. In October 2005 the Lozells and East Handsworth area, where white residents are a small minority, witnessed a seriously destructive, riotous conflict between Afro-Caribbean and Asian residents, following the circulation of a rumour that a black woman had been raped by Asian men. These events, and their associated territorial and cultural affiliations and assumptions, are an important aspect of the experience of the young people of the West Midlands. They are reflected in the life of the project whose history we are unfolding.

The target and the actual Ballet Hoo population

Two hundred and twenty young people, rather fewer than the planned 300 envisaged by the Ballet Hoo! contract, turned up for the four day intensive YAR-led training sessions which took place in May and June 2005. To what extent did the 220 participants fit the profile of young person the Ballet Hoo! project aimed to attract in its original specification.

The Ballet Hoo! contract laid down that the young people taking part should be at least 15 and no more than 18 years of age. An independent evaluation of the project written in late 2006 makes it clear that the programme was for 'disadvantaged' or `at risk' young people in this age group, and YAR, as its name indicates, aims to work with young people who, however one likes to put it, have problems or are in trouble. However, the contract between YAR and the four local authorities at no stage used the terms 'at risk' or 'disadvantaged', neither did it indicate the sort of 'problems' the young people might have or identify the kind of 'trouble' they might be in. The contract simply described a 'youth development' programme and then, in an appendix entitled 'Participant Enrolment Policy', identified various categories of young people whose characteristics or behaviour would make them unsuitable on the grounds that, though wishing to be inclusive, "we feel we could not manage [them] safely and beneficially". That is, only the excluded were identified. These categories were young people:

- physically dependent on (addicted to) drugs/substances eg heroin, cocaine, alcohol, 'skunk weed';
- with a Statement of Special Educational Needs, which identifies significant learning difficulties, in the mild, moderate or severe range (usually this corresponds to an overall IQ of <70) who are likely to be too challenged by the intellectual component of the programme coursework;
- with severe impairments in communicating (receptive and expressive difficulties, such as severe language delay, autism, mutism)

- with significant sensory impairments, such as profound visual or hearing impairments, likely to seriously limit involvement in certain aspects of the programme;
- with significant medical problems requiring specialist interventions which may put the young person at risk on the intensive residential programme and/or which might/does profoundly affect mobility or consciousness. Moreover, it was additionally indicated that:- "for us to exercise our duty of care responsibly, we would need to give careful consideration as to the suitability for our programme of young people:

- with a history of, or currently suffering from, major mental disorders, such as psychotic episodes, schizophreniform or affective (bi-polar) psychoses, incapacitating obsessive compulsive disorder, severe panic disorder, current severe acute or post-traumatic stress disorder;
- with neurological conditions potentially affecting mobility or consciousness (eg. epilepsies);
- using medication which is causing significant sedation or inco-ordination;
- currently in established psychotherapeutic relationships."

In all of the above cases "we would require the support of and written consent from the young person's responsible medical doctor, consultant psychiatrist or therapist".

This list of unsuitable potential participants may appear restrictive – indeed both Michelle Bould, the Sandwell project co-ordinator, and Ali Reilly, from Dudley Black Country Connexions, were initially concerned about the apparent exclusion of drug users. But if disadvantaged was the general target criterion, consider the candidates who could in fact be included. Young people in trouble by virtue of their offending behaviour and subject to a criminal court order were not excluded. A high proportion of young people use illicit drugs or drink alcohol to excess, but cannot reasonably be described as physically dependent or addicted: thus occasional, recreational illicit drug users were not, as Michelle and Ali understood the matter, excluded. Also eligible were young people temporarily or permanently excluded from school, regularly not attending or poorly achieving. Looked after young people, a group which successive research reports have shown to be generally vulnerable and severely under achieving, were also not excluded. Nor were young people not in education, employment or training – the so-called NEETS – or those living in severely deprived households or neighbourhoods. It follows that most young people with whom youth workers work and who would be judged disadvantaged were eligible.

There was good reason to unambiguously specify groups who would not be suitable. This was a physically demanding dance project. If there was to be any prospect of success, it was going to be reliant on tight discipline, good physical co-ordination and the ability to follow instructions closely. Furthermore, the YAR method is by common consent fairly difficult. It uses unfamiliar language and a lot of "chalk and talk". It requires participants to think clearly and communicate their thoughts. Though the approach emphasises trust, safety, support and love, and though it is in principle backed up by a life coach framework, it would have been irresponsible to take on adolescents in the volatile throes of drug addiction or severe mental instability: the life coaches, in particular, with their modest training, could not have been expected to cope with young people with those characteristics.

As we will see problems arose in the early stages of the project with regard to recruiting, training and retaining the local authority 'trailblazers' whose principal task was to identify suitable young people for the project. Of the 65 youth workers who originally agreed to become trailblazers, only 30 helped out in the enrolment process. The consequence was that that task was tackled in different ways in each of the four local authorities and more of the work was undertaken by the project co-ordinators and Black Country Connexions staff than was originally envisaged. It was they who got to know the majority of young people best and who were looked to by most of the young people as advisors, mentors and trusted friends throughout the remainder of the project. If 'disadvantaged' was the recruitment criterion, albeit that term was never defined, then Sandwell arguably stuck to the original brief most closely. Michelle

Bould, the Sandwell co-ordinator, originally trained as a dancer and before joining the local authority team had worked as an education officer with BRB. While with BRB she had gone to deprived areas in Birmingham to recruit young people for their dance summer schools. At the time of her secondment to the Ballet Hoo project she was working part time as the Arts Development Officer for Sandwell Council. She, possibly more than anyone else on the local authority side of the project, was able from the beginning to appreciate the demands that would be made of the young people. Sandwell enrolled 68 young people, more than their allocation of 50,

social services care team, pupil referral units, special and other schools, Black Country Connexions, youth clubs, and so on.

In Dudley, Ali Reilly, a trained social worker for Black Country Connexions with no previous experience of arts projects, did the bulk of the enrolments. It was mostly done through two secondary schools where there were significant numbers of young people 'at risk', and through referrals, notably from Connexions. Fred Richings, the Dudley co-ordinator whose previous role was as Dudley Council's arts officer, reports that no Dudley referrals came through the local youth service, a particularly interesting fact given the Chief Executive, Andrew Sparke's, aim of changing the culture of his youth service. It would appear that the Dudley Youth Service was at this stage wary of the project and effectively declined to get involved. Dudley enrolled their young people by these means and though Ali steadfastly looked for young people at risk, she confesses that it did not always turn out that way

because some of her local intermediaries nominated a number of young people who, despite her clear advice, were not greatly, if at all, 'at risk'. Wolverhampton recruited largely, though not exclusively, through two secondary schools with highly disadvantaged catchment areas. But here the approach was different from that in Dudley. Most of the young people contacted and subsequently enrolled were already engaged in the performing arts, particularly dance. That is, they mostly had prior involvement in performing arts education courses or such activities through school clubs. A good many were not identified as being individually 'at risk' or personally 'disadvantaged'.

Birmingham arguably strayed furthest from the planned enrolment and interview process, which was largely due to the operational problems outlined in the next chapter.

In Dudley, Sandwell and Wolverhampton practically every young person attended a presentation

outlining the project and all those enrolled were interviewed and assessed during a two hour process which had previously been developed with YAR. The process encouraged the young person to talk about and discuss where they felt "they were" in relation to their life and general welfare. The purpose was to identify significant issues affecting them at the time of enrolment and how they felt about these. Part of this process involved asking the young people to identify three 'life goals' for themselves, aims that were designed subsequently to guide the work of the life coaches with them. This process also ensured that these three local authorities built a set of records which enabled, among other things, the independent evaluator commissioned subsequently by the partners to the project, to write a report which was fairly comprehensive in its coverage. In Birmingham, however, the hiatus regarding the appointment of a project co-ordinator, the absence of effective local line management and the loss of most of the trailblazers, meant that enrolment was done mostly through community-based youth clubs and with young people already involved in the performing arts. The assessment was cut to a brief ten to twenty minute process and few records remain. The consequences of these initial short cuts were evident throughout the project for several Birmingham participants. It showed in their lack of understanding about the nature of the project and their life goals, their lack of conformity with ground rules and the poor quality of their relationships, where any relationship existed, with life coaches. These

shortcomings were significantly counter-balanced, however, by the very strong, supportive relationships which many of the Birmingham young people developed with the tardily appointed Birmingham project co-ordinator, Denzil Peart. This was particularly true during Phase Two of the project and Denzil continues to maintain a powerfully supportive relationship with many of the Ballet Hoo graduates even though he is no longer employed by the local authority.

At Risk or Not At Risk

The asymmetric nature of the Ballet Hoo recruitment process within the four local authorities raises an interesting question. Were the Ballet Hoo participants 'disadvantaged' or 'at risk' and to the extent that, by default, they were not, was that a project weakness or, ultimately, a project strength?

It is clear that most of the Ballet Hoo participants were by any standard individually disadvantaged, though they may not have recognised the fact. Consider the following sample of anonymised pen pictures, recorded (in

different styles, depending on their trailblazer or local project co-ordinator) at enrolment:
'X has been in care from the age of eight. She currently lives with long-term foster parents. She is known at school under the name of Y (her foster carers' name) but plans to change her family name by deed poll in the near future. Her foster parents are very supportive of her participating in the project. X attends Z school regularly though she has been excluded several times for aggressive and disruptive behaviour. She has recently been given an educational mentor organised through Education Support Services

(for Looked After Children). Her grades have as a result begun to improve as has her general behaviour. She is 15 and about to enter her final year at school. X's three life goals were: quit smoking; change my attitudes towards my parents, foster parents and school; and do well in life (people say I won't)

'T is 18, lives with his elderly parents and attends U College, a college for 16-21 year olds with special needs (particularly autism). Although T is dyslexic and his literacy skills are very poor, he is a very gifted artist (particularly cartoons) and loves acting. He is a very reflective young man and tries to makes sense of the world around him. This means that he sometimes asks what appear to be bizarre questions, but they always have a point. This

makes him vulnerable to bullying until people get to know him. He will need support to express himself confidently and negotiate the complexities of peer relationships (he doesn't have many friends). T's life goals were: improve my art/drama skills; improve my general health and fitness; and blend in with people.'

'K is 15 and was enrolled through his youth offending team and is subject to a court order. Has run away from home twice. Wants to re-build relations with his father. Is currently being looked after by his aunt. Past history of serious physical child abuse. Violent and complex family life. Has anger management issues. K's life goals were: get closer to Dad; and improve relations at home with his family.'

A is 16 and has been in care since she was 14. This was as a result of her father raping her. She receives a service from the 16+ Team (for looked after children) and will do so until she is 21. A has recently (temporarily) moved back with her mother (following the break up of a violent relationship) but will be moving into her own accommodation shortly. A will be starting at B College in September to do a two year course in Art and Design. She would like to become a fashion designer. A's three life goals were: listen to people; control my temper; and start eating healthily.'

'G is 18 and was enrolled through a local arts centre where he practiced his break-dancing. He is unemployed and has no educational qualifications.

He says he was bullied at school and then became a bully, was de-motivated and has low self-confidence and self-esteem. He says he alleviates his boredom through drinking heavily and walking the streets looking for trouble. He was attracted to the project because of the Channel 4 connection and is interested in ballet because it might improve his suppleness, which would help his break-dancing and sports. His life goals were: meet new people; be healthier; be more flexible physically.'

'M is 16 and lives with her mother, who suffers from bouts of depression. Her older brother recently moved out and this has made things less stressful in the home. M sees her relationship with her mother as sometimes being role reversed: that is, she

has to parent her Mum. When things get too stressful between M and her Mum she goes to her aunt for a few days until things have calmed down. M is starting at N College in September to do three A Levels. She is quite apprehensive about the transition. Stress seems to be quite a dominant feature in M's life and she struggles to keep focused when things are overwhelming her. She manages her stress through self-harm, in particular cutting herself on her arms and the tops of her legs. M's three life goals were: handle my emotions and stress better; have a healthier diet; and have better communication with my family.'

Many issues were uncovered in the course of enrolment. Michelle Bould, the Sandwell co-ordinator, reports that 20 per cent of the young people she enrolled resulted in new child protection cases (everyone was warned at the outset of their enrolment interviews that if they said things which prompted serious concerns for their safety, the matter would have to be reported to the relevant authorities). This means that serious

matters came to light of which social services, schools and youth offending teams were unaware.

Michelle says that she heard of things that were horrifying and which will never leave her – for example, accounts of sexual abuse and other forms of violence. She had sleepless nights over what she heard. Some of the revelations were bizarrely shocking. To illustrate the point she recalls a girl who like many of her colleagues identified 'stopping smoking' as one of her apparently straightforward life goals. When asked why she had prioritised that particular goal she answered, again apparently conventionally, that she had started smoking rather early. When asked, how early? she answered 'When I was four: my Mum used to put a lighted cigarette in my mouth because she thought it looked cool.' Now aged 15 she was acutely addicted to nicotine such that she couldn't concentrate in school for more than fifteen minutes: she needed a fag. Despite the fact that most of the young people from Wolverhampton and Birmingham were recruited through their existing

involvement in performing arts activities in schools or youth centres, many of them also had major problems, whether or not those issues were fully appreciated by those who enrolled them at the time they enrolled them. Yet it is also clear that a good many of the young people from Birmingham and Wolverhampton were not particularly disadvantaged individually, albeit they were overwhelmingly working class in origin, lived in predominantly working class neighbourhoods, went mostly to school in large inner-city comprehensive schools and a high proportion of them – 45 per cent – were from minority ethnic communities or were of mixed race. The point is this. The Ballet Hoo! cohort was perhaps not the concentrated, multiply disadvantaged, seriously high risk youth group some youth workers thought it should be. Given that the project cost a good deal of money, some of the staff involved felt, that had the cohort been more clearly disadvantaged then the project would have added more value. No one agrees what proportion of the Ballet Hoo! cohort was drawn from

outside the disadvantaged or `at risk' target group: estimates range from one or two young people to 10-15 percent depending on the commentator's perspective. What is clear is that a number of young people were recruited to the project who, everyone agrees, were creatively thriving without the benefit of the Ballet Hoo! leg-up. But would the project have been so resounding a success if some members of the cohort had not been the successful, positive, stabilising influence they were – role models, in effect - and if more participants had been wracked with the negative consequences of deeply troubled personal lives? This question is incapable of being answered definitively but connects to broader philosophical questions which lie at the heart of a debate within the arts community about how best to work with young people at risk. The irony is that by administrative default the Ballet Hoo! cohort

conformed more to the mixed model favoured by Stephen Ball of the Birmingham Repertory Company, who refused to take part (see Chapter Three), than that designed by YAR and the project co-ordinators.

Ab's story

I first arranged to interview Ab and her brother S in autumn 2007, but they never turned up at the Leaps & Bounds offices where it had been arranged I should meet them. Then in January 2008 I got Ab on the telephone and we arranged to meet at her flat in a week's time on a day when she said she wouldn't have to be at college. The day before I was due to meet her I rang her to confirm the arrangement. She had forgotten our appointment, apologised profusely when she realised she couldn't make it, and agreed instead to meet me, again at her flat, in the afternoon of the following day. I arrived at her flat on

time. There was no one at home. I rang her on her mobile. She was in Wolverhampton. She wasn't going to be able to meet me. Things had not gone as expected at college in the morning. She was with her Mum. The car they were in had broken down. Assistance had taken a long time to arrange. And so on. She was once again profusely apologetic. I told her I would ring the following day and see if we could do all the talking we needed to do on the phone. Which is how I eventually got to talk to Ab who, very regretfully, I never met. I would have liked to. She sounded really bubbly and positive on the phone and, disarmingly, admitted

that 'time management' was not her strength!

I'm 20 and I've lived most of my life in the West Midlands, though for a period I went with my Mum to live in Devon. I've had my own flat for a while now - arranged by the 16 Plus Social Services team - and I'm doing an Art and Design degree course at the University of Wolverhampton. I want to be designer when I've finished my course, but I'm not sure what sort of design. I've just learnt how to 'tuft' rugs and at the moment I'm really excited about the idea of rug design. But over the next two and a half years I expect I'll learn lots of design skills, so I don't know what I'll end up doing. I'm just determined to do well in my course, graduate and get a job in design.

I was born in Wordsley in the Black Country, not that far from where I now live in Stourbridge. My brother S, who was born just under a

year after me, also lives nearby – so we're very close together in age and experience.

I don't remember it but my Dad was very abusive to my mother when S and I were small babies. My Mum's told me, for example, that when I was teething and wouldn't stop crying, my Dad was so angry that he picked me up and just kept shouting and shaking me. That's a really dangerous thing to do: babies have died because of being shaken. And he was violent to my Mum. Once he pushed a bottle in her face and wouldn't take her to hospital, so she had to get there herself. And he beat her. But my Mum wouldn't tell people who'd done it to her until, in the end, social services got involved. Mum had a nervous breakdown. My parents split up. And S and me were taken into care when I was three.

Between the age of three and ten S and me lived with foster parents. We had three

or four different ones. Most of the time we were together. It was good and bad. Our first foster parents, with whom we stayed for about two or three years, were brilliant. They were amazingly good to us and I'm not sure why we got moved from them. But the second couple we were with were horrible, particularly to me. They wanted my brother. They even wanted to adopt him. But they didn't like or want me. I remember one morning I was sick into my porridge and the man asked the woman what he should do. She told him to stir it all up and make me eat it. And he did. It was like that. I was only about six and tried to tell social services that I didn't want to stay with them, but we weren't moved from there for almost two years.

By this time Mum had sorted herself out and was fighting to get S and me back. But it took her a long time and it wasn't until I was ten that S and me went back to live

with my mother. She had a new partner by then and over the next few years I got three more brothers, step-brothers, though I think of them as full brothers. But my Mum's new partner, C, started sexually abusing me when I was about 12 or 13. I didn't realise it was abuse at the time. I thought it was just cuddling. But he used to ask me to lie on the sofa and he'd put his hands up my top. He told me not to wear a bra when I was in bed. And he'd give me 'special cuddles' when he'd had a bath. He was also abusive to my mother, though not physically like my Dad. But he used to shout a lot and he wouldn't let her do things. Social services didn't do anything about any of these things until my mother had a nervous breakdown. C's abuse of me didn't go further than the things I've said, but it was abuse and he was eventually taken to court, though he got off. In the end Mum decided that she had to escape from C and we all went to live in

Barnstable, Devon, where I first went to secondary school. I liked it in Barnstaple. I had lots of friends there, but when I was 15 we all came back to Wordsley and I had to go to a different school.

It didn't work out and I didn't do well in my GCSEs – mostly Ds or Es – largely because I hadn't been going to school much of the time. There was a particular teacher who shouted at me a lot and made me unhappy. So I bunked off and after I'd taken my GCSEs I left. In S's case it was worse: he got expelled from school, though he did take some GCSEs. I did a lot of different things after I left school. I started a hairdressing apprenticeship course, but packed it in after about two months. The working conditions were dreadful – there were several fires in the premises - and I had to work long hours for very little money. Then I did a drama course at Dudley College for a month or two. Then I started an Arts and Design Course at Halesowen. This went really well. I liked the course and got distinctions and merits

for my work. For some of the time I combined it with working at a dental technician workshop where they made moulds for teeth and things.

I didn't stay living with my Mum and my brothers and sister. Mum had a small house and it was pretty crowded. So, it was arranged for Stan and me to move out and have a small flat together. It was while we were there that we learnt about the Ballet Hoo project. I think I was referred by my care worker to Ali Reilly in Connexions. I was interviewed with S. at the Netherton Arts Centre. We were told it was going to involve a ballet and would conclude with a performance at the Hippodrome and that we'd have lots of opportunities to learn different things, including –and that's what particularly interested me – designing costumes, theatre sets and other aspects of production. I was asked what life goals I'd like to set myself and I think I said I wanted to be more confident, manage my time (I'm pretty bad at that) and

stick to things better.
I remember the four-day intensive course at the beginning of the project. It was led by a woman, Denise, who at first I thought was really crazy. She told us all about the problems she'd had in her life and then expected us to talk about ourselves. She said that if we weren't able to talk about the issues in our lives then we'd probably never get to deal with them. It was hard. But I gradually got to understand some of the things she was on about and though I didn't really want to talk about myself in front of everyone, in the end I did, though I was cautious about what I talked about. Some of the other people talked about really sensitive things and we all ended up crying. I didn't do that. But I did say quite a lot about myself and not until I'd done it did I realise how important it was to have done it. I felt loads better afterwards. I don't know to what extent my brother talked about himself in his group – they put us in different groups for the four-day intensive – nor what he talked about if he did open up. But I learnt from the

exercise. It made me think more about the choices I had to make and the need for commitment and how, if I want things, I can make things happen. I found the whole thing useful and unlike some of the people, I didn't have any problem with the ground rules they set. You've got to have rules.

After the four-day intensive I took part in the programme of activities and enjoyed them. But I missed quite a few sessions. I found it difficult fitting everything in. In fact it was all too much. So I didn't take part in the performance at the Drum Theatre in early 2006 and though I opted to start Phase Two of the programme, I dropped out of it shortly afterwards. Several things were going on at the time. I was doing my course. I wasn't that interested in dance and taking part in the ballet – it's not really my thing: I was always more interested in the production side of it and there wasn't

much scope for involvement in that. And then early in 2006 my Mum took me and S. to meet my Dad, who still lives in the Black Country and who we hadn't met since we were small children. That was very revealing. He just wasn't bothered, had no interest in us at all. That affected S. more than me: it upset him. And meeting my Dad made me realise how much my Mum had cared for us and what she'd done for us. I appreciate that better now. Finally, Ali, who, though she wasn't officially my life coach, became my life coach in the sense that I consulted her and she helped me a lot, didn't try to make me stick with the programme. She said it was important that I followed my own goals and if that meant leaving the project, that was fine. So I did leave the project. As did S. at about the same time.

I think I would have left the project whatever had happened in spring 2006, though I'm not sure about S. who was badly affected by meeting our Dad again. But I wasn't really interested in ballet and wanted to get on with my design course. And I felt I'd got a lot out of the project as a result of the personal development side of it. It proved really positive for me. I don't think S got as much out of it as me. He dropped out of the same college course that I completed. He's working at Somerfields now. We used to have a flat together, but he's living now with a friend and I've got my own place.

I didn't go to the Hippodrome performance. I'm not sure why. I think I must have been doing something else at the time. But I did see the TV series, though there was only a very brief shot with me in it in one of the early programmes. I thought the tv series was brilliant. You could see people growing during the project. I think I grew as a result of it.

chapter 5

'crisis and credibility'

Multi-agency partnership working involves the meeting of different languages, philosophies, working assumptions and undertakings. The Ballet Hoo! partners represented all these differences in spades. There were also significant power and status issues for the partners who were well aware that the project was taking place under the lights and lenses of television cameras. Reputations were on the line.

MUCH   ASK **THE LEAPS & BOUNDS STORY**

71

At the outset, the likely benefits seemed to outweigh the possible risks, but as soon as the project began philosophical differences emerged and organisational pitfalls began to appear.

In January 2005 a two day stakeholders kick-off workshop had been held to ensure that the partners understood the repercussions of what they were signing up to.

A YAR discussion device – 'the menu and the meal' – was employed to explore what everyone considered they were letting themselves in for, and how they might react if the project didn't quite turn out as they expected. Which options could and might they choose in the event of their being disappointed? Were they going to send the meal back? Or complain? Or would they eat it, albeit reluctantly. By these means, basic agreements were worked out as to what it was that all parties were committed to delivering, come what may. For the project co-ordinators this was their first experience of YARs working methods and they were impressed. What they admit, however, is that at that stage they could not envisage what those working methods would look like when applied to the young people.

The results from the stakeholders' kick-off workshop were written up. Nevertheless, even the best laid plans hit unanticipated snags of which personal doubts and lack of commitment are possibly the most corrosive. Not everyone liked core aspects of the project methodology and in May 2005 a crisis blew up which threatened the project. It emerged that key BRB staff had fundamental doubts about the acceptability of YAR's methods.

By late May 2005 the first four-day intensive training sessions for the enrolled young people had been completed, most of the sessions being witnessed from the back of the room by the project co-ordinators, trailblazers and the key representatives from BRB, who at a later stage would be responsible for the dance training. It was at this point that one or two of these observers expressed serious reservations about YAR's methods. Given that all the staff had themselves undergone YAR training two or three months earlier, how could this be?

The two four day intensive training sessions with the young people held in May 2005 were indeed intense and occasionally highly emotional. Very personal revelations were made by some of the young people, revelations occasionally accompanied by tears. This process of opening up was explicitly encouraged by the trainers. There were also a few conflicts, mostly involving young people breaching procedural rules to which, at the outset, they had agreed. When such conflicts occurred they were not backed away from. They were confronted, firmly. The young people were reminded what they had signed up to. The trainers made it absolutely clear that the agreements and rules were going to be enforced.

The process was inclusive, but it was also tough. Issues were not left unresolved. Non-engagement was not tolerated. It was made clear that if the young people were to take part, they had fully to take part. There were to be no free-riders, no silent passengers, no creeping out of the room when the going got tough and people found it convenient. This was a group process where everyone was going to learn from everyone else. That meant that the participants really had to get to know about themselves and each other. All of which meant that from time to time the experience was uncomfortable and disturbing for everyone, including the observers.

Personal scars were exposed, unwillingness to participate was challenged, anger was expressed.

Such events are often more difficult to observe than to participate in. Furthermore the "faster" training sessions for adult professionals tend to be more low-key, more emotionally controlled and personally less challenging than those for young people. Adult professionals are typically more confident and guarded and, unsurprisingly, the YAR trainers tended not to push into their personal space. With young people the tensions tend to be nearer the surface, relationships more volatile. They are often less secure than adults or have built up

fewer or less robust defensive walls around their insecurities. Anne Gallagher, the Director of Education at BRB for example, says that not until she observed the first YAR sessions with the young people, did she fully appreciate what was involved and the possible implications. It was not, she is at pains to emphasise, that she was uncomfortable about working with disadvantaged or difficult young people; she was highly committed to that prospect – indeed she had previously been closely involved in a BRB Birmingham Schools project. What she questioned was the manner in which it was proposed to work with the young people.

It is YAR's rule that observation at group sessions is permitted, but the observers must at the beginning say who they are and thereafter strictly observe silence, sitting behind the group participants who all face the trainer. The observers must not intervene. They do not take part. It follows that when things become emotional some observers instinctively wish to jump in and rescue, particularly if they also feel that emotionally charged issues are best held in. Outward signs of pain are, after all, inconsistent with the typically controlled, stiff-upper-lip, reserve which is one of the hallmarks of the British cultural tradition.

One or two of the adult observers back in spring 2005 found the experience of watching the youth training sessions sufficiently disturbing that they requested an emergency meeting with Neil Wragg. The first such meeting happened on 16 May. Anne Gallagher, BRB's Director of Education was the prime mover. At the meeting she expressed concerns about the tough manner in which the YAR trainer had dealt with some of the young people at the first intensive training session. In response Neil stressed the importance of setting clear boundaries. If the young people were going to be able to rehearse effectively and perform a classical ballet, they would have to be sufficiently disciplined to follow instructions and be consistently accountable for their behaviour, even when they didn't much feel like it. Rigour had to be established from the outset.

Other partner concerns were also expressed about organisational shortcomings. Contractual undertakings were not being fulfilled. The dire shortage of life coaches was mentioned, but the concerns mostly related to Birmingham Council staff who stood accused of unprofessionalism, an ironic situation given the Ballet's longstanding partnership with the City and their general inclination that Birmingham should have been the lead authority for the project. It was said that despite repeated promises, paperwork giving parental

consent for the young people's participation had still not been completed. It was stressed that no physical dance work could take place without such consent.

When the 16 May meeting closed Anne Gallagher said that she was much more at ease with the project. But if that was the case her ease did not last long and her and others' concerns deepened. Further observations of the ongoing intensive training sessions led her to express doubts about the professional integrity of YAR as an organisation. She says that her reservations were shared by colleagues from the BRB education team, one of whom said that she wouldn't care for her teenage daughter to be involved. She challenged the acceptability of YAR's methods and called into question the involvement of YAR in the project. She says that she thought it inappropriate for the young people to be pressed or encouraged to reveal issues in their lives which were intensely personal and sometimes sensitive, particularly given that everything was being filmed and these revelations might subsequently be shown on television. Further, she was not persuaded by the argument that the young people, and their parents, had consented to the process. She doubted whether the young people were sufficiently mature to appreciate the possible long-term consequences of their decisions and she considered that most parents, not having witnessed the method, would not have understood what it was they they were signing up for. Anne telephoned people around the country who she understood had some knowledge about YAR to try and find out more about the organisation. She recalled that she had rung me at the Youth Justice Board, something I had forgotten. She said she received both enthusiastically positive and negative reports. My own view, based almost entirely on my sheep-dip experience at Chartridge, (see Chapter Two) she described as 'balanced'. She persisted with her objections. A second emergency meeting was called for early June 2005.

The meeting was chaired by a BRB trustee and attended by all the principal players from the local authorities, BRB and Diverse Productions, who had been filming the four day intensive programmes. Neil Wragg from YAR was, in effect, put on the stand at the insistence of one or two critics. Neil, knowing that this was a critical moment, prepared carefully for the ordeal, acknowledging that he and his colleagues at YAR had probably taken too much for granted. That is, they'd got the project off the ground with agencies and persons who had little or no prior knowledge of YAR. They had assumed that the three day training delivered at the beginning of 2005 for all the key professional staff with whom they were now working had provided sufficient explanation about what they were about. They thought their credibility had been established. It was now clear that this was a mistake. YAR's bona fides had not been established, at least not with everyone. In retrospect, Neil's view is essentially endorsed by Anne Gallagher. She says that she failed to ask questions about YAR and its methodology that she should have asked at the outset. She also says that she did not think through the implications, principally the risks, of having the TV cameras in.

Prior to the meeting, Neil consulted a few members of YAR's advisory group and within a day or two his office had put together a 20 page report for discussion at the emergency meeting. The report addressed the concerns principally being expressed by Anne Gallagher, and Yousiff Meah, Head of Birmingham's Youth Service. The concerns were about YAR's methodology and the management of the project to date. Some of Yousiff's Birmingham trailblazers were reportedly not participating because they considered YAR's training approach tantamount to bullying. This idea had gained momentum following the dramatic walk-out by several Birmingham youth workers from the trailblazers' training back in January: one youth worker had resented being required to wear a name badge and the rule, routinely enforced, of standing when speaking during sessions. Others objected to the requirement that they remove their hats.

Anne Gallagher's concerns were such that she wanted to be present for the entirety of one of the four-day intensive programmes and wished to bring with her the Ballet's consultant psychologist to observe. These were powerful voices.

The report prepared by YAR unequivocally opened with an apology: insufficient work had been done by YAR to explain to everyone the relevance and safety of the organisation's approach. The report set out to repair this gap. It explained that since it's foundation in 1992 YAR had delivered more than 200 programmes to more than 3,500 young people, 2,500 professional staff and 2,500 volunteers. Several appraisals of the organisation's work were cited:

'It (YAR) has, in a relatively short time, generated the degree of identification, loyalty and commitment by those involved in the best of voluntary organisations. This

is because Youth at Risk has proved that it can make a significant difference to the lives of disturbed young people with whom others had failed, and demonstrate that all young people have the potential to make a constructive contribution to their society – given the opportunity.' (John Huskins, formerly HM Inspector for Youth Services, 1996)
The West Belfast Youth at Risk pilot programme has demonstrated that it is possible for even the most alienated and disaffected young people to radically change the direction of their lives and begin to make a positive contribution to their community. The young people who participated in the programme were believed to be beyond help. Intervention by statutory agencies and the local community had made no impact on their anti-social behaviour prior to the Youth at Risk programme.' (Independent evaluation undertaken by the University of Oxford of a YAR Coaching

for Communities programme, 1999) 'Youth at Risk has a strong philosophy and set of aims that are very relevant to the national agenda to promote social inclusion: Youth at Risk successfully promotes young people's self-esteem and supports them in bringing about change in their lifestyle and relationships.' (Ofsted Inspection Report, 2001)

The report provided a very brief technical summary of the theoretical foundations for YAR's modular training approach – 'Gestalt theory and Rogerian reflective therapy combined with a Socratic approach to encourage reflective questioning'. This description may or may not have been meaningful to all those reading it. Possibly anticipating incomprehension the authors helpfully summarised in colloquial terms their approach as: 'challenging, compassionate and based on the belief that

people are 'able' rather than 'disabled'. An example being that most young people can read and write at some level and Youth at Risk engages with that rather than 'you can't'. A simple description is 'tough love'. Clear boundaries and absolute support.

Youth at Risk is not a youth work agency, nor is it social work or strictly therapy. Rather it provides an opportunity for individuals to reflect on their lives, and for them to see and build a future for themselves – which they would not have considered possible had it not been for the YAR training.'

Appendices to the report provided impressive lists of notable people who had participated in YAR training courses or were trustees or members of the organisation's Advisory Board.

The report also honestly accepted that although

feedback on YAR's training programmes overwhelmingly comprised 'good' or 'excellent' comments; it was still frequently the case that 10 per cent of participants returned 'poor' or 'very poor' evaluations. Neil Wragg emphasised that YAR aimed to learn from these minority negative views and from any programme which failed to achieve generally positive outcomes. He also emphasised that in 12 years YAR had never previously been charged with bullying and not once had they been the subject of a complaint of not treating young people safely.

The second half of the report chronicled the history of the Ballet Hoo! project and progress to date. It was conceded that everything had not gone according to plan. The failure of the life coach recruitment process was detailed. An insufficient number of life coaches had been recruited and those that were, had not been

trained and put in place early enough to meet the needs of the young people. By November 2004, part-time project co-ordinators had been appointed in Dudley, Sandwell and Wolverhampton. But in Birmingham it was decided that the full-time co-ordinator post would be job-shared. It was also decided, arguably reflecting a misunderstanding as to the purpose and nature of the project, that the operation would be managed by the Arts and Leisure Directorate as opposed to the Youth Service Directorate. This decision was predictably to skew the profile of the Birmingham young people subsequently enrolled.

The Birmingham job-share co-ordinator arrangement did not work out. One incumbent was almost immediately away from her desk long term for personal family reasons. The other incumbent had only a few weeks of her fixed-term contract left to run, failed to

get her contract extended and departed for another job. There followed an hiatus of almost two months during the critical set-up, training and recruitment months of February and March 2005. Moreover the Birmingham senior managers, from both the Youth Service and Arts and Leisure Directorates, only intermittently attended the Partners Steering Group. The two departments also fought. Birmingham's financial contribution to Ballet Hoo! of £150,000 was taken out of its Youth Service budget, but Arts and Leisure was given lead responsibility to administer

the project. This decision was resented by the Youth Service Directorate who understandably sought to retain some control over how their money was being spent. Meanwhile, Birmingham's Chief Executive did not engage with the project and indeed Neil Wragg never met her. The consequence, as we have seen, was that very few Birmingham trailblazers were recruited and fewer still remained active by the time Denzil Peart was appointed long-term project co-ordinator in April 2005.

There had been two 'trailblazer' training events,

one in January 2005 with 49 participants, two thirds of them from the Black Country, and another in the following March with 16 participants. This was well short of the 80 trailblazers specified in the contract, Birmingham accounting for most of the shortfall. Further, though the evaluation feedback from the training sessions was overwhelmingly positive – 78 and 94 per cent respectively of the participants rating the training good or excellent (the rather conspicuous walk-out by one Birmingham youth worker thus being an exception) – a significant proportion of the recruits

subsequently declined to take on the trailblazer role. The most common reason was that the extent of the commitment involved had not been explained to them prior to the training. Only 11 trailblazers participated in a 'youth enrolment training' event arranged over two days in March, though a greater number worked with the Black Country project co-ordinators to actually undertake the enrolment process. When Denzil Peart was eventually appointed at Birmingham, there were only three or four trailblazers left for him to work with to find and enrol the formidable target of 150 young people

Birmingham had been allocated. It is scarcely surprising, therefore, that in the end far fewer young people from Birmingham took part in the initial intensive four day training programme compared to those enrolled from Dudley, Sandwell and Wolverhampton.

Neil Wragg describes the 16 June meeting as the most difficult he has had to undertake since becoming YAR's Chief Executive in 1994. The meeting lasted half a day. He did not feel looked after by the BRB trustee who chaired the meeting: instead of being impartial, Neil felt the trustee saw her responsibility as backing Anne Gallagher, a senior employee of the company.

Having introduced evidence about his organisation's history and professional integrity and having reported the overwhelmingly positive feedback from the training provided to the project's professional partners in January 2005, Neil found Anne Gallagher's continued objections unreasonable. He felt angry. He could not see what more he could say. He was grateful, therefore, when Michael Waldman, Diverse Productions' director for the filming of the project, intervened with a question which broke the log jam. Michael bluntly asked Anne what more YAR could do to persuade her that they were a professional organisation with whom she could comfortably work for the safe benefit of the young people concerned. She replied that there was "nothing" they could do. Whereupon Michael asked how then could she lead a BRB team who the evidence suggested generally did

have confidence in YAR. Michael Waldman thereby made the disagreement a personal issue.

Anne Gallagher recalls a subsequent discussion within BRB in which it was made clear to her and her colleagues that if YAR was not a partner then Diverse would pull out and the TV commission from Channel 4 be lost. Despite her reservations it was decided the partnership with YAR and Diverse had to go on. However, Anne also believes that had it not been for the tie-in with Diverse and Channel 4, BRB would have pulled out at this point. She concedes, however, that her reservations about YAR's methodology were not shared by the BRB artistic staff who were to be most involved in the project, Desmond Kelly and Marian Tait.

In addition to these threats to the project, there was much behind-the-scenes wrangling between Anne Gallagher and Dudley Council over Keith Horsfall's responsibilities in running the

project. Anne had from the outset questioned the allocation of the overall direction of the project to an officer of Dudley Council and Keith felt his role was constantly being undermined. It was no secret that some BRB staff would have preferred BRB to have joint management of the project with Birmingham City Council.

In the absence of Andrew Sparke, Keith Horsfall chaired several of the early meetings of the Partners Steering Group. He found the meetings so awful that he dreaded them, not sleeping or eating beforehand. He questioned whether he had been promoted a step too far and was up to the job. The representatives of all the agencies were successful people in their own spheres. So they were very confident and sometimes dogmatically assertive when seated at the communal table. Keith recalls taking his dog for a walk one night and wrestling with the stances taken by the different partners. What was the project for? Was it about regenerating deprived neighbourhoods and their young inhabitants? Was it about creating a good publicity tv series? Was it about efficiently delivering a social inclusion project for the Arts Council? Was it about the Black Country local authorities challenging the dominance of Birmingham? Was it about in-service training for staff and changing the ethos of the youth service?

Keith's Eureka moment came from what he'd started to learn about the young people they were enrolling. He knew that some of them were facing hell in their personal lives. He decided that the bottom line, which had to be the basis of every solution to every argument, was: would it improve the life chances, without serious risk of harm, of the individual young people involved? If they were convinced it would, they'd do it: if they were not convinced, they wouldn't.

In the event the organisational rubbing point which existed between Anne Gallagher and Keith Horsfall and the YAR staff was

resolved by Anne obtaining a fellowship to undertake an arts leadership course. She was granted a year's sabbatical from November 2005. From June until her departure in November she says she "gritted her teeth" and got on with the organisational job required of her. But her doubts were not dispelled. She agrees that the September 2006 performance which marked the conclusion of the project was 'brilliant' and a 'phenomenal achievement' having watched the film of it in America. But she does not think the successful performance removes the basis of her doubts. First, she does not know how important the YAR group sessions were to the success of the project. Secondly, she wonders what happened to the young people who, as she puts it, 'dropped out' and did not take part in the final performance. How many of them were discomforted by the YAR process and turned off by it? How many casualties were there? These are issues to which we will return in the next chapter.
Anne was replaced by Ginnie Wollaston as BRB's

Education Director, an arrangement that everyone considers worked well. Yousiff Meah, Director of Birmingham City Council's Youth Service, also moved on in the sense that he had no further involvement in the project. In effect, the doubters took themselves off and were replaced by enthusiastic participants who made the project happen. Most, though not all, of the co-ordinators and other front-line workers were stimulated and excited by YAR's approach with the young people. Michelle Bould, for example, emphasises that there is no way she would have sanctioned use of a method she considered dangerous or risky for her young charges. She found her own assumptions about youth work refreshingly challenged. Some of her colleagues were 'blown away' by the sessions. Others began by being highly sceptical, wondering, in the words of one of them, 'What the fuck are they talking about?' and 'How on earth am I going to recruit young people to come along and listen to four days of this stuff?'. But within a few hours or days they were won over by the

persuasive argument that the core of the method involved not letting young people get away with excuses for bad behaviour and not colluding with them – a process damaging to the young people themselves and others. Ali Reilly, for example, recognised that in her professional practice she had done precisely that – in the past colluded with the unacceptable. She, like her colleagues, was converted.

Settling to the Task: Partnership Working

Almost everyone involved in the Ballet Hoo! project has one or two searing memories from spring 2005. It was an exciting and stimulating period. But it was also tense and uncomfortable. YAR had taken on a project on a larger scale than anything they had previously attempted. They were also working in the cultural field of ballet, which was unknown to them. The four local authorities had never worked in such a partnership previously. Many of the local authority staff – particularly Keith Horsfall, the Project Director, and his local authority assistants and co-ordinators, Denzil Peart in Birmingham, Fred Richings in Dudley, Michelle Bould in Sandwell, Ian Wright in Wolverhampton, and Rachel Alston and Ali Reilly from Black Country Connexions, were new to organisational tasks of this complexity: they had to learn by doing. Finally the BRB staff, the local authority project co-ordinators and trailblazers were confronted by YAR's methods, which were not just unfamiliar, but to some extent culturally foreign, 'in your face', and disturbing.

One or two players doubted the roles they had been given and called into question the plot as a whole. These conflicts were not in the end calamitous. They were for the most part dealt with calmly and diplomatically because the key players – Neil Wragg from YAR, Andrew Sparke in Dudley, David Bintley the Artistic Director at BRB - had the vision to see a long-term outcome from which everyone could benefit. Their leadership was vital because their vision prevailed. Further, the second tier people whose enthusiasm and commitment was critical because they were to have the first-hand dealings with the young people – the Project Director and the local authority project co-ordinators, the principal YAR trainers, Will Daniel-Braham, and Beki Martin, and last but not least the Artistic Director and Ballet Mistress, Desmond Kelly and Marion Tait – were all sold on it. Which is not to say that none of them entertained doubts about aspects of YAR's methodology and some of the organisational features of the project, particularly the fact that it was to be televised. Most of them initially had serious doubts. But they were soon persuaded that the overall package was inspiring and convinced that it could be made to work.

By the end of July 2005, 220 young people from the four local authorities had been recruited and had turned up for the four day intensive training courses led by YAR. This was well short of the target of 300 young people stated in the local authorities' contract with YAR, but it was nonetheless a sizeable venture.

The presence of cameras. Diverse Productions, and the tie-up with Channel 4, was part of the project from the outset. That nonetheless left open questions about what was to be filmed and what should be included in the television series which, in the final analysis, comprised three hour-long programmes of fly-on-the-wall footage of the eighteen month programme, and an hour and a half-long presentation of the concluding Hippodrome performance. The Ballet Hoo! team were convinced that the TV tie in was a fantastic opportunity: for the young people to show what they could achieve, thereby potentially enhancing their career prospects; for YAR to demonstrate the transforming potency of their method; for the local authorities to exhibit their innovatory capacity; and for BRB to show off professional excellence and their outward-facing, non-elitist, social inclusion credentials. But everyone was also conscious of the risks. The exercise might backfire. Individuals or agencies might be revealed as incompetent. Professional standards might not always be maintained. So-called partnerships might turn out to be destructive jousting matches. And, most of all, the young people might during the personal development sessions reveal aspects of their lives that it would not be in either their or their family's best interests to be known to the public at large. Everything hinged on whether the TV team could be trusted to respect the interests of the parties involved.

Roy Ackerman, the Director of Diverse Productions, was known to have had a long association with YAR and from his statements and reputation was trusted as a responsible producer of high quality documentaries. But like YAR's Neil Wragg, Roy was operationally distanced from the project. Convincing the people on the ground was a task that lay more in the hands of Michael Waldman, the series producer and director and Claire Lasko, the director and producer of the programmes. Claire was in charge of day-to-day filming and was the person who the rest of the Ballet Hoo! team got to know best.

Everyone appreciated that if the tv series was going to be a success it would have to be entertaining and the film-makers would need to develop identifiable characters and story-lines. It was also likely that binary sequels would be fixed upon: the transformation of individuals – from unsuccessful to successful, uncommitted to committed, ill-disciplined to disciplined, not achieving to achieving, bad to good. It was a question of balance. How far was it acceptable to reveal the negative end of the spectrum, and would the

exceptional incident be highlighted to achieve sensational contrast? Claire Lasko was the person who by common consent convinced the rest of the Ballet Hoo! team of Diverse Production's integrity and commitment to the underlying aims of the project – enhancing the prospects of the young people. Claire, it was felt, could be trusted: she became one of the team. The perception was that if there was a choice between showing more or less sensational contrasts in order to make the tv series more interesting to viewers, Claire would always err on the side of protecting the interests of the individuals involved. She wouldn't always have her way in Diverse Production team discussions, but she would ensure that the integrity of the project, and the individuals involved, was protected.

It is nevertheless apparent that the Diverse Productions team exerted a powerful influence in the decisions as to which young people got key parts in the final Romeo and Julia production. Where several candidates were suitable or able, those young people whose statements or

revelations during the YAR-led personal development sessions were most dramatic were singled out by the film team as potentially interesting character story lines, and their views were clearly communicated, albeit sotto voce, to the project co-ordinators and BRB team. But the Ballet Hoo! team as a whole appreciated that the tv series would have to have entertainment value and that this sort of selection was a reasonable request and price to be paid for the publicity benefits they judged would accrue.

Secondly, it was agreed that if members of the Ballet Hoo! team felt that a filmed revelation, conversation or incident should not be used in the series, they should say so from the outset, and such requests would be requested. What could not happen was for objections to be made at a late stage, when the film team was a long way down the track editing the material, though individual young people and their parents still had that right.

In the event, as we shall see, meetings were held during the course of the project with individual parents or carers to ensure that they

were willing for difficult personal revelations to be aired (see, for example S's story). Not everyone was entirely happy with all aspects of the programme and many of the young people disapproved of the degree to which 'bad' behaviour was portrayed. But the general view is that Diverse Productions fully honoured their agreements and did justice to the aims of the project. Moreover, no one disputes that the original hope, that all aspects of the project would be put on the map by virtue of the tv series, was fully realised. The tv series is almost universally judged to have been a great success.

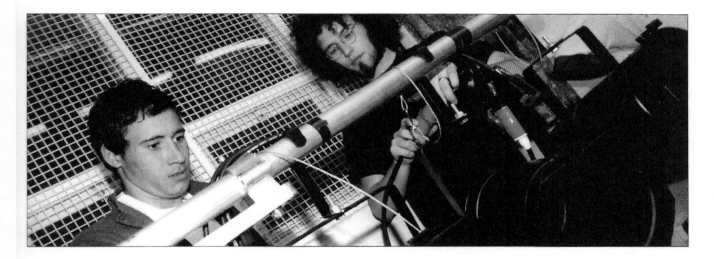

C's Story

I met C in a Cotswold Boarding School – Sibford School at Sibford Ferris near Banbury. Sibford Ferris is little more than a hamlet, set in glorious, rolling countryside, at the centre of which is the school. It was autumn half-term and the school campus was almost deserted apart from one or two administrative staff and workmen renovating a teaching block. C is both a member of staff and a student at the school. On the day I met her she was there with her mother and a niece and nephew, her sister's children, visiting her over half term week. How C, who comes from Washwood Heath, Birmingham, and has lived most of her life there, comes now to be a student at a Quaker boarding school in the Cotswolds, where the fees for boarders are in excess of £6000 per term, is a miraculous story worth the telling. Her mother sat with us while C told me the story.

How do I come to be here? Claire, one of the directors from the Ballet Hoo project has a friend, Maggie Guy, who is Deputy Head here at Sibford. Claire invited Maggie and her husband and children to come to the Ballet Hoo show at the Hippodrome. Maggie saw me perform and I assume asked Claire questions about me and the project. I was subsequently contacted and offered a scholarship. So, two months after the Hippodrome performance I started at Sibford and it's planned that I should be here until summer 2008. I'm doing a B Tech, which is equivalent to an AS Level, in Sport.

Most of the Sibford students are from well-off backgrounds.

Some of them come from wealthy and even famous families. But you wouldn't know it from talking to them. They're lovely people. Everyone at Sibford is treated as an equal. I've never felt out of place here. Had I felt like that I would have left by now. I don't think I'm the only student with a scholarship. But there's no one else from my sort of background. The school offered a place to X but she was still doing her GCSEs. Maggie Guy has told me that the school would like to offer a scholarship place to a participant of the Leaps & Bounds project on a regular basis.

Sibford School approached me through Denzil [Denzil Peart, the Ballet Hoo co-ordinator for Birmingham], who was almost more excited about the idea than I was. But he didn't have any details. So at that stage I didn't know what the offer was. Whether it was to come here as a student, or during a gap year or as a member of staff. But then Claire explained that it was a scholarship to do a B Tech in Sport and to combine that studentship with being a member of staff. So I do classes with the students and I help supervise some activities as a member of staff. I don't have to pay fees and I get paid. I work as a lifeguard in the swimming pool, for example. At 20, I'm two years older than the oldest students, but that's not a big difference. I don't feel awkward about it. It works very well.

I was born in Birmingham, so I'm a Brummie, though I know I don't have a typical Brummie accent. That's because my family is Irish, so I have a bit of twang. I've got two older brothers and one older sister. My Mum and Dad split up when

I was about nine. Initially we all lived with my Dad. But later on I moved between them, spending time with each of them more or less equally. They live close to each other, only about two miles apart. And I also stayed with other members of the family, aunts and uncles, in Leicester and other places.

I went to primary school in Tile Cross, which is further east out of Birmingham than Washwood Heath, between Washwood Heath and Birmingham Airport. I liked primary school, I was happy and got on fine. I learned to read and write, I went regularly and I made friends. But after I left, at the age of 11, even though I had been allocated to Archbishop Grimshaw Catholic School in Chelmsley Wood, I never went. It wasn't that I was feeling rebellious, I just got out of going to school. I made a decision not to go, and I didn't go. I know it sounds strange. But in my sort of Irish family, going to school isn't top of the list. It's not a priority. We've got a lot of family, and you travel round your family. School gets sort of shoved into the background. My brothers and sister went to Archbishop Grimshaw, though they didn't stay into the sixth form – they all left. But I never went at all, and I suppose the authorities never did anything about it because of my living at several addresses and moving about between them. I sort of slipped through the net. [At this point I asked C's mother, who was sitting listening, whether she was worried at the time – when C was 11, 12, 13 that she wasn't going to school. She said: No, because as she said we were moving from family to family, from one sister to another sister – I've got a lot of sisters – so she was always with adults and there was a lot going on at the time.]

I spent my time with the family. My Mum's one of twenty children. So we went from town to town. There was always someone to go and see. And you do a lot of baby sitting, stuff like that. You've got to be in a family like mine to understand it. When I was 12 and 13, becoming a teenager, I was happy not going to school as anyone that age is happy not to have to go to school. It was cool. But, though I still didn't think I was missing out, by the time I got to 14 and 15 I started thinking that I was taking something away from myself. I didn't blame anyone, because it had been my decision not to go to school. But at age 16 I did start to think that if I was going to get into college or something like that, I was going to need some GCSEs – which I didn't have. I wanted now to do something more than what I was doing. So I went to the local Connexions centre in Tile Cross, which is the area I always go back to. I sat down with a gentleman called Gary Coffee and told him the whole story. I doubt he had ever encountered someone like me, because he was surprised. He agreed

with me that I needed some basic English and Maths. I'd kept up with reading – magazines, things like that. But my spelling had slipped. He suggested that I go to a training centre in Tile Cross called Three Es. And I did, though it took about three months to arrange. I started there in January 2004 and did English, Maths, Arts, Citizenship, stuff like that. The other young people at the training centre were the same age as me and had for various reasons dropped out of school. Then, when I was nearly finished at the training school - I'd been there for almost a year - I got involved in the Ballet Hoo project. Denzil came with a woman from the film company.

Denzil gave us a bit of a run-down about what the project was all about and asked us to fill in a form. There wasn't really an interview. He just chatted to us for a bit so that he got to know us. About ten or twelve people from the training centre were approached. He explained that it was going to be on TV and would involve ballet. He didn't say too much about the personal development side because I suppose he thought that wouldn't be too inviting. When me and my friends saw the cameras we

went 'Yes, yes!'. That was what attracted us – that we'd be on TV in eighteen months time. I told my Mum and Dad about it and they were very supportive.

I went to the place where the initial four-day intensive training took place with three friends from the training centre. We were all white, and the rest of the group we met at the centre were predominantly black. I was used to that. Washwood Heath is a very mixed area – all races, black, Asian and so on. However, I remember wondering: 'Where did they go to, to get all these people?' because we had thought that it was just going to be us and few more. We had no idea how big it was going to get.

The group was led by Denise and Will. Both really nice people. I got to know Will a lot. They were trying to get us all to open up within four very intensive days. I'd never encountered anything like it before, It was quite different. But some people played up to the life coaches and the cameras.

I didn't have any problem with the ground rules. It was a very mixed group. Some people were happy. Some

were unhappy. Some had problems. Some had bad tempers. I remember one time they had us sitting there for over an hour and we were losing our heads in this room. People were saying 'Can we go out please? Can I go and get a drink of water?', and they wouldn't let us. That was one bad memory I had. They kept us sitting for too long. It was Mark. He was holding a cup and saying 'A cup is not a cup. It's only a cup in conversation.' He dragged it on for too long. So a lot of the kids felt 'If they're going to keep us sitting there for that long blabbing on about things we don't understand, then I'm not doing this.' So, quite a lot of people dropped out quite quickly. I understood most of the things they were getting at. But you know how it is. If someone's trying to explain something to you and you get it a little bit, and then they try to explain a bit more, and a bit more, you reach a point when it's going over you. You shut it out.

I think they were trying generally to get us to understand that we could talk about it, whatever it was. And that they would be there for us. That they weren't going to get us to open a can of worms, and then let us deal with it on our own. Some kids opened up, and some kids didn't. They tended to focus on people who had a story to tell and wanted to tell it. Kids who put their hands up. They didn't victimise people. And people tended to be in little groups. I was with my three friends from the training centre. And we were quite quiet. We made friends with everyone and we were respectful. We were older than most of the other kids, and perhaps more mature. So when we saw other kids playing up, we thought we didn't need to add to the situation, so we didn't say so much. I did say something to the whole group – we all did. But I didn't reveal much about myself. I only did that to people I trusted, individually. Some people revealed very personal things, and I thought that was OK because I knew there would be support for them afterwards. The people I didn't understand were those who said that they hated all the personal development stuff and kept playing up, but kept coming back. I suppose it took them longer to learn things.

They were trying to teach us basic things, like punctuality. Never be late for anything. Be respectful. And you can make things happen. You can realise your life goals. I had earlier said that my life goals were: be on time, because I often wasn't; stop smoking – I'd started at about 14 and I wanted to be fit for the physical things that I knew I was going to have to do; and get on a course, which I did.

After I'd joined the Ballet Hoo project I started a B Tech Diploma in Sport, which is the equivalent of a GCSE, at Bourneville College. I was fit. I hadn't done sport formally as you would in school. But with two older brothers I'd always played football, and I had a passion for it. I'd never been in a team, I'd just gone with it. Even so, I didn't finish the Bournville course. I only did half of it, for six months. I was one of only two girls in the class and I didn't like two of the staff. I thought they favoured the boys and it was really hard for me and this other girl to be in that environment. After that I was just job-seeking. I didn't look very hard. Maybe I was being a bit lazy. I was with my Mum and the Ballet Hoo project came first with me. I didn't get a job until after the Hippodrome performance.

All four us from the Tile Cross training centre stayed with the project into Phase Two. But only two of us took part in the performance. One of my friends dropped out because she was a bit on the heavy side and felt self-conscious about it. She didn't think she'd look good with the other girls when she was dancing. Her life coach tried to help her get over this, but she couldn't. The other one dropped out because she was given only a very small part, and I think she thought that it wasn't worth the effort.

I'd never done dancing before, at least not properly. And I'd never been to the ballet, though I did go to a play when I was in primary school. I thought of ballet as someone prancing about in a little pink skirt. But when you see it close up, you realise it's completely different. It's really athletic and professional. You want to get involved in it. Even the music. When I used to hear classical music, I used to think 'Get that off'. Now it's not like that. Now I listen to classical music in my lessons: I put it on as background. You open your mind to things. During the project I was introduced to things that I'd never experienced before and never thought I'd be interested in.

At the beginning of Phase Two we started going to the rehearsal room at the Birmingham Royal Ballet. Marion [Marion Tait, the BRB Ballet Mistress] put all us girls through the various acts and decided who was best for the different roles. I was one of two allocated the part of the nurse. When I heard 'C – nurse' I thought 'This is massive. What am I doing? I won't be with the group now, I'll be more on my own.' But I thought I could handle it. I just wondered whether Marian was going to be able to bring this character out of me, because I'd never done any acting before. whereas the other girl who was allocated the part had done drama lessons. So I knew that if I was going to do it, I was going to have give 110%. In the event the other girl wasn't able to do it, because she moved to London. However, even after the other girl left they didn't say to me, 'You are the nurse.' They left me with the impression that they could get one of the professional dancers to play the part. So I had to continue giving 100% and I came to think that the part was mine. By the time it came to the performance, I felt the part was mine.

I doubt I will ever again have the feeling I had on the night of the performance. It was amazing. The rush I got from going out on the stage for my first scene was fantastic. But it was over too quick – almost in the blink of an eye.

I had a big downwards feeling the next day. It was like, now what? The project had dominated my life for 18 months. And now it was over. I felt that I was losing friends and things like that. It was a sad time for several weeks.

I started a job, as an old people's carer, a few days after the Hippodrome show. And shortly after I started the job I heard through Denzil about the approach from Sibford School. My life coach, Sushila Patel, also called me about it. I'd got quite close to both Denzil and Sushila. Denzil was in authority, but he was also a mate. And Sushila was very supportive to me, helped me to organise myself, particularly during Phase Two. I'm still in touch with Sushila, in fact it was her who first brought me to Sibford, to see the place.

The tv series was and wasn't what I expected. I knew that they were going to develop certain people so that they had a story. So I expected that. But I was surprised that

they showed as much of the rude, disrespectful, time-wasting behaviour that they did. The staff and the project didn't deserve that. There were some kids who were on the project but sort of not on the project: there but not there. I suppose they showed the bad stuff to get the viewing and get across the message that 'ballet did change my life'. [At this point C's Mum said how interesting she had found the programmes. As she put it: C only missed out on not going to school. But some of the kids came from terrible backgrounds] It was a shock seeing myself – but a pleasant shock. For the final performance I was pleased how professional I looked – it was what I'd been aiming for. I was nervous. But I was nervous to get out there and

do it. It was the high point of my life so far – without any doubt.

My concentration now is on getting top grades here at Sibford. I'm getting good marks, so I feel I've caught up. I don't think I shall have finished studying when I leave Sibford. This course has given me the route into going to college, to university. So I should like to consider doing a sports psychology course or something on those lines.

During Ballet Hoo I grew up – as did a lot of the kids. It was life changing. It helped me develop life skills. It made me believe that if you've got the will, if you've got the commitment, you can achieve things. If I'd been offered the chance to come to Sibford before the Ballet Hoo project, I wouldn't have come – no way. It would have seemed too scarey. I wouldn't have thought I could cope. Now I can.

When we had finished talking, C showed me her room, to the side of the common room on the ground floor of the student accommodation block where she lives. She had two small rooms, the walls decorated with family photographs. On the top of the TV, was a photograph, from the Hippodrome performance of Romeo and Juliet, of herself on stage as the nurse together with the ballerina who played Juliet.

My concentration now is on getting top grades

chapter 6

'how was it for you?'

During the last weekend of June 2007, Ali Reilly and Michelle Bould arranged for over thirty Ballet Hoo! graduates to come together at a Black Country retreat to reflect on their experience of the project.

Will Daniel-Braham, one of the leading YAR trainers, Denzil Peart, former Birmingham project co-ordinator now working on his own account, and Michael Waldman from Diverse Productions were also present. Several of the sessions were filmed, it then being hoped that a Channel 4 follow-up programme might be commissioned. The primary purpose, however, was to help me gather the young people's voices in preparation for this account.

It was a wet but chaotically festive weekend (the nearby Severn was severely flooded downstream). Though many of the young people had individually been in touch with each other during the preceding nine months, this was the first time that so many Ballet Hoo! graduates from the four local authorities of Dudley, Sandwell, Birmingham and Wolverhampton had come together since the Hippodrome performance on 28 September 2006. The

camp staff were used to catering for cub-scouts, and found it difficult to accommodate exuberant, boisterous 16-19 year olds intent on having a reunion party. For my own part I departed on Sunday afternoon exhausted, not least from lack of sleep. The aim had been to get the young people to write about themselves and their experiences, in retrospect a naïve hope. But the weekend was nonetheless valuable. It enabled me to gather a range of views about Ballet Hoo! and to build a sufficiently firm foundation to subsequently visit a selection of those present and interview them individually. The purpose of this chapter is to explore in greater detail than has been explained so far how the project was received by the young people it was designed to serve.

Recruitment and Enrolment

Recruitment and enrolment to Ballet Hoo! took roughly

the intended course in the three Black Country authorities but, because of trailblazer difficulties and the late appointment of a project co-ordinator, short cuts were taken in Birmingham. A substantial questionnaire form entitled 'Where am I now?' had been devised by YAR for candidates to complete. The same form, very marginally tweaked, is being used for the Leaps & Bounds follow-on projects. Contact details, family history and current relationships, life-style and health issues are covered. The final pages record life goals and the reasons for choosing them. The nature of the Ballet Hoo! Project was explained and the young person encouraged to talk in depth about themselves. Consent forms were signed by both the young people and their parents or carers. If followed to the letter the whole process typically took two to three hours.

It is clear that however the

young people heard about Ballet Hoo!, the fact that a TV appearance was in prospect, with a performance at the Hippodrome at the end of it, was a major draw. Yet a large proportion were attracted simply by the fact that it was a dance or drama project. They'd either been involved in such artistic endeavours before and wanted to do more, or found the idea intrinsically appealing. It was dance rather than ballet which was the attraction and many of them associated the activity with being fit or becoming fitter. The overwhelming majority of all the young people enrolled in Ballet Hoo! mentioned wishing to pursue a healthy lifestyle, becoming fit, stopping smoking or losing weight as one or more of their three life goals. Health is a major preoccupation among this age group.

Several of the young people offered a more personal or philosophical explanation of their decision to get involved. Someone from Sandwell, for example, said: "The thing that made me apply was that I saw this as a new beginning. This could be the one challenge that could help me to understand myself and to rebuild broken relationships."

Recollections of the enrolment and interview process vary. Some young people say it was "boring" and "involved a lot of paperwork". More typical, however, is the early appreciation of the fact that the project wasn't going to be like school: they had to talk about themselves. One youth recalled having "to tell a complete stranger… about my inner secrets and emotions and problems (about) which I was very shy at the time". Another remembered "walking into a room and being asked various questions" which he described as "emotional for him, but the beginning of trust…. a new beginning in my life and coming to term with some of the problems I faced." One girl said "We had to bare all on our personal lives and speak in depth about our personal experiences". Another recalled "having to tell people stuff about myself,

things they wouldn't have expected to hear from me".

Those who stayed with Ballet Hoo! to the end (the graduates) are generally those most likely to have got to know one or other of the Leaps & Bounds staff team well and in that sense they are not representative of the 220 enrolled. Even so it is striking that many of the young people report the importance of particular key workers involved in their enrolment. Denzil Peart, Ali Reilly and Michelle Bould were all repeatedly mentioned as individuals who they liked and whose presence clearly attracted them to join the project. Michelle's contention that the mere fact that an adult not in authority spends two to three hours non-judgementally listening to the candidates' analysis of their life situation is of itself a benefit to the young people.

Some, however, were cautious at the enrolment stage. A girl who was to reveal a great deal about herself during the personal development training recalled "being quite reserved during the enrolment process and wary about what I was signing up for". Another girl

remembered Michelle, who she thought "really nice", explaining that the project "would help build our confidence" but also "told me that if I really wanted to come and join it I would have to be more open". In this respect enrolment was, as it was designed to be, a preparation for the YAR programme.

Youth At Risk Intensive Personal Development Training

The YAR group process is grounded, as we have seen, on firm, participatory ground rules which the young people contracted to abide by during the enrolment process. The training

modules that YAR trainers use mostly take the form of 'conversations' about 'distinctions'. The aim is to get the young people to appreciate that there is a difference between the essence of something and its conventional appearance, between how things (persons or events) are described and how they really are, between fatalism and possibilism, and so on. These exercises or 'conversations' are difficult. They touch on major philosophical questions. As we saw earlier, Keith Horsfall, the Ballet Hoo! Director, confessed to not grasping some of it (see Chapter Two). How then in 2007 did the young people

remember the initial four day intensive training sessions held two years previously?

A good many simply recalled that the sessions comprised 'conversations', many of them about 'life goals' and that there was a lot of "talking and sitting down". The recollections were sometimes acerbic. One girl, for example, remembered "Will's 'conversation' about a flipping chair, which was totally irrelevant to me!" It is clear that some of the exercises had gone over many heads. One youth found them "confusing… because they were speaking a different form of language which was alien to me". One young person recalled:

"Having to wake up early and get a taxi to Birmingham to go to the session. I was very nervous about talking. I couldn't understand half of it. Will said things and I thought 'What the hell is he on about?' It might have helped the others, but it confused me. I'm intelligent in some ways, but not in others. When asked to say things I lost track of things. I was glad I wasn't portrayed in the TV film."

Most, however, recalled gradually getting into things. One youth wrote:
"I thought – WOOO!!! What the fuck is this about? I saw the tall American black woman and thought I was on Oprah Winfrey. But then I

relaxed a lot."

In many of the sessions the young people were passed a cup to hold when speaking. Where the cup might be passed next had for many been a source of considerable anxiety.

One girl remembered:
"The conversation cup. I always jumped out of my chair to go to the toilet. I could never just sit there and handle it. But towards the end I started to listen and it has helped me."

One youth recalled that it was:
"Tiring. Mrs Spaghetti hair [one of the black trainers]. Being coached due to my

and X's attitude. But I felt better once I shared my problems. Some things were personal, like my friend committing suicide – leaving me depressed and upset. But I gained confidence because people didn't judge me. I could open myself up."

A girl wrote:

"I remember being in a hall with around 20 other young people. Denise, who was taking our session, went around the whole room and asked people 'to step out of their fear' and share their problem. I was shocked to discover some people's problems and what they had been through. When it came to my turn I was lost for words and found my problems were nothing to what the others had said."

participants rated the information they had been given to be excellent or good (67 per cent), likewise the location and quality of the training (80 and 87 per cent respectively) and even more telling were the responses about what they had learned. Eighty six percent gave the highest ratings to the question as to whether they had learned something new about themselves. Almost as many, 81 per cent, reported having learned something new about the situations they were in. Eighty nine per cent said they now saw new choices open to them and 88 per cent reported having learned new skills. Similar numbers said the training had been made relevant to them and that they had been supported by fellow participants. Nine out of ten rated the whole experience excellent or good: that is, the 'conversations' worked.

This was clearly a prominent aspect of the learning – hearing that others were experiencing issues similar to oneself or, apparently, far worse. Several of the young people talked about this. No matter what the benefits of hearing each other's stories may have been for shaping their own decisions and aspirations, it was clearly significant for bonding the group and thus an important ingredient in the subsequent teamwork they were collectively able to achieve. Empathy was built and trust developed. This comes through strongly in several of the young people's stories.

Those young people who during the reflective weekend offered me rather stark, negative one-liners about the

initial YAR sessions (such as "crap" and "boring") offered more considered, positive appraisals when individually pressed. It seems likely that because, over the eighteen months of the Ballet Hoo! project, they had internalised much of the YAR approach, they'd forgotten or did not appreciate the degree to which their thinking had in fact developed. Certainly their accounts are at odds with what the staff say of their progression. Moreover, the feedback collected by the YAR team immediately after the four day intensive sessions looks very different from what some of the young people now say in retrospect. Analysis of 116 written appraisals returned following three of the courses show that the overwhelming majority of the

One girl wrote:
"I remember the trainer explaining that we are the 'players' in our lives and the way we played our game was influenced by the past and which also then affected the present."

Others commented:
"I felt that I was thrown in at the deep end as far as the personal development aspects of the intensive, but towards the end of day two I felt more at ease in what I was being told and what I was learning."

"Uummm… getting up at 4 every morning… having to stand up in front of everyone and say who I am which was hard because I was so shy… but I loved it."

Which is to say that the gain was often accompanied by discomfort if not pain. There was in fact a lot of discomfort, but YAR does not pretend that the process can be undertaken without it.

It is unclear, however, as to the degree to which the fact, that some of the participating young people were not 'at risk' or particularly disadvantaged may account for the annoyance that some

participants felt about being pressurised into revealing problems they felt they didn't have, or exposing matters best kept private.

One youth said:
'I did it, but I found it offensive – being told, made, to stand up and say things. It was embarrassing. I didn't mind doing it myself. But I thought it was offensive the way he [Will] treated the other people.'

One of the young people made a strong statement of this viewpoint: Will and the other trainers were "bastards" who "kept trying to create issues" where, by implication, there were none.

My own impression, having talked at length to several of the young people, is that this issue is related more to the fact that many of the young people, though faced with problems or disadvantages in their lives which most people would consider major, often did not see them as such. They saw many of the issues to be part of what they regarded as normal, their accepted lot in life. Thus to suggest that their situations were abnormal, problematical, requiring change and so on, was, they felt, patronising or

it was insulting to call into question their personal integrity and social dignity. This impression comes through very strongly from several of the young people's stories. This is the fine line which the YAR approach treads: how to challenge the lives of young people who in many respects have settled, or are inclined to settle, to their less than perfect situations?

The four day intensives involved more than the YAR training. BRB provided a short dance exhibition which many of the young people recalled as important. One youth said the display "made me question whether I could do the impossible". There was also a drama workshop which, as S's story makes clear, proved to be a turning point for her. Another girl recalled "we got to meet new people and express the way we felt through dance". Two of her colleagues described "the dance and drama [were the] best parts of the day" and "brilliant". Another, who had been dismissive about the YAR sessions, referred to "loads of other activities they had done on ballet and getting to know each other". Indeed 'getting to know each other' was for many the best part

of the experience, though others mentioned the food, which had apparently been worth getting up for in the morning.

We cannot leave this topic without mentioning the fact that the initial training sessions were filmed and several dramatic, revelatory episodes from them were prominent in the tv series. Many of the young people, as we shall see, objected to aspects of the tv series, but none thought that any of the revelations, whether used for the tv series or not, had been damaging to those participants who made them. The Ballet Hoo! staff agree. One can argue as to whether some of the revelations were exploited for entertainment purposes. Different views are held on this topic, as are contentions as to whether it was justified. But no one considers that any harm was done and most of the young people and staff argue that this was the inevitable price one has to pay for all the positive publicity which the TV series generated to practically everyone's benefit.

The Follow Through Programme

The Phase One follow-through programme took place after the initial personal development training from September 2005 through to March 2006. All the young people met together for an activity programme for one Saturday or Sunday a month, the design of the programme having been suggested by YAR and broadly accepted and arranged by the local authority project co-ordinators.

The aims of the follow-through programme were to:

- introduce the young people to the resources available within their community;
- challenge stereotypical views of young people and encourage the community to see them in new ways, and vice versa;
- support the young people in going beyond where they would normally stop;
- get the young people ready for Phase 2;

- raise the young people's aspirations;
- deal with other everyday issues such as conflict resolution, remedying mistakes, improving communication, gaining commitment, etc.
- support the young people to achieve their life goals.

Young people who did not positively engage with the programme were still considered to be on it, since there was always the possibility that a change of heart could occur. The co-ordinators and life coaches tried to keep in touch with and re-engage the approximately 60 absentees from the number initially enrolled. A 'Refresh Report' was commissioned to look into disengagement. A number of absentees were interviewed and the results were far from negative. Some were honest enough to admit that they had simply not made any effort – to get out of bed at the weekend, for example. But significant numbers felt that they had benefited from whatever

involvement they had had to date. For example, of the enrolment or personal development training, several said :

"Bit scared at first then I started doing a lot of talking and feel quite proud of myself for attending and setting goals"

"Made me want to achieve [my goals] even more"

"Felt like a chance to build a great career, instead made new aspirations"

"Attendance helped build up my confidence"

"I know I got to help myself – It woke me up"

Only one in five of the absentees was negative about the experience – "I don't know really – was boring, not my thing" - and others explained their absence for difficult, practical reasons - "I've been kicked out my Dad's place - I won't be able to do it". There were also

examples of disengagement for very sensible, positive reasons. For example, one 16 year old single mother, pregnant again but in a stable relationship with the father of her child, reported having enrolled in college to pursue a Business Studies course. She kept in touch with the project and attended the final Hippodrome performance.

Nonetheless it seems probable that several organisational factors contributed to disengagement. First, was the shortage of life coaches. Second, was the difficulty of maintaining momentum due to the long gaps, in some cases weeks or a month or two, between enrolment and intensive personal development training, between the intensive training and the first follow-through weekend workshops and, if the young people missed a session, between the weekend workshops themselves. This also frustrated the life coaches, particularly those living at a distance from their mentees. The Refresh Report stressed the importance of early life coach recruitment and tight timescales, lessons the Leaps & Bounds team have learned for future projects.

A third problem was the fact that BRB, jealous of their artistic role, insisted that there be no discussion of Romeo and Juliet or any dance workshops unless BRB organised them for the group. This was particularly frustrating for the considerable number of young people whose motivation in signing up was dance-related. Some threatened to leave the project. The problem was eventually remedied firstly by the project co-ordinators organising their own, contemporary dance sessions and secondly by BRB contributing to weekend workshops in late 2005. Two dancers from the company led ballet sessions, working alongside several freelance contemporary dance teachers as part of the Sunday activity carousels. BRB began with introductory sessions on the style and basic vocabulary of ballet and took this further during the intensive dance-led activity from January to March 2006. The project co-ordinators organised three small area showings of work over Christmas 2005 to keep the motivation of the young people alive.

The first intensive weekend workshop took place in February 2006, at Birmingham Dance Exchange, where the creativity of the young people was given its head. There was a shift of emphasis towards developing dance skills; the young people began to work more closely with BRB in developing their contemporary and ballet skills and learning scenes from the ballet. This was followed up with a lecture demonstration by David Bintley, Artistic Director of BRB. The young people then went to the Hippodrome to watch a public performance of ballet. Some of the dancers they had met were performing. Desmond Kelly and Marion Tait led a discussion which took place immediately after the performance. The young people were reportedly 'blown away' by what they saw.

In March 2006 there was a performance of "work in progress" at the Drum Theatre, Aston, Birmingham.

The invited audience comprised friends and family and those involved in delivering and supporting the project. This was a successful and demanding event. The young people got a glimpse of the future demands that would be placed upon them in Phase Two of the project. The Drum Theatre show, unlike that at the Hippodrome, provided some participants with the opportunity to undertake front-of-house (technical) rather than performing roles.

"I didn't perform because I always perform that kind of dance and within theatre there is more than one side so I wanted to experience that."

"I took a role on the technical side and became stage manager as I wasn't comfortable dancing. I had the vital role of making sure everything was on cue and ready. I really enjoyed this role and felt more comfortable doing this than performing."

For the overwhelming majority of the performers the Drum experience was exhilarating, even transformative – a prelude to what was later to happen at the Hippodrome.

"It was amazing – a large audience and a proper performance. I didn't dance but sang songs with my band. I got great feedback and complements. It boosted my confidence drastically."

"It was good. Pure energy. Everyone put in 100%. A sick show."

"I took part. It was a combination of break-dancing, body-popping and street dance. I feel this performance showcased us young people's personalities through dance. I felt very proud that I had come so far

in such little time."

"Before the show I was very nervous. But when performing it felt like I was born to perform. And when we had all gone home it was like I had no life in me. All my energy had gone."

Even when respondents had had prior performing experience the Drum Show appears to have been very rewarding, though some realised they had a way to go:

"It was fantastic even though I had performed on a stage bigger with more audience than that before. It felt like a different experience – and I liked it!"

"At the time I thought it was amazing and felt proud of it. After watching it on DVD I realised it wasn't as good as I thought and that I would have to vastly improve for the ballet performance."

To celebrate the end of Phase One a celebration

evening was held for everyone. Jamelia, a national pop figure, was the star attraction. Certificates were handed out to all Phase One participants. The young people were then given a choice (always part of the plan) of whether to continue or leave the project. It was made clear that Phase Two would involve far greater pressure and time commitment. Given that Phase Two would for some participants run alongside GCSEs and college examinations, some declined to continue. For the more 'at risk' young people, however, the project was often the only event in their lives: it became increasingly important to them as they made new friends and a clear goal was in sight for them to aim at.

A similar choice was given to the life coaches, some of whom felt that the demands of the programme made it difficult for them to sustain their commitment alongside the rest of their lives. Thirty

life coaches agreed to continue in support of 82 young people during Phase Two.

The participants who continued into Phase Two were, not surprisingly, very positive about what they had gained so far. They were more confident, they had made a lot of new friends and they had got into or improved their dance. Some felt they had developed in other ways.

"I felt a great sense of self and reassurance. I had learnt so much about my own way of thinking and how I did things. I also realised that there was a lot about myself that needed to change, and I am glad that I have."

"I felt I had started to build on my confidence and the person I was inside. I felt more open minded and ready to approach new things. I also felt better able to deal with new situations that come up."

"I felt somewhat glad that Phase One had finished, but I could not wait until Phase Two began because I knew that Phase Two was going to ask more from me - in terms of both mental health and physically. I knew I had to be ready."

"I got the sense that something was going to come out of the project. I realised that a lot of people from my comfort zone were dropping out and that I had to start speaking to more people from different areas."

Their motivations inevitably varied, depending on why they had first enrolled. They wanted more of the same, whatever the same was:

"A chance to do bigger things."

"Work towards the end result [the performance at the Hippodrome] that would be a once-in-a-lifetime experience."

"I wanted to be able to say I had completed something. I'd previously dropped out of a few things."

"To get somewhere in life. Before Ballet Hoo I got into trouble a lot, got into fights, robbing, etc. I was hoping the project would turn my life around and that I would better myself. It did help me achieve this. Without the project I would have been stuck."

"I hoped to achieve, this time to be on stage, not just in the background, on the technical side. This I knew would be challenging, and I had to really consider whether it would be achievable. But I decided to go ahead with it.... and I achieved my goal."

"I wanted to see if we as a company could pull it off, and to see what it involved as it sounded as if the heat was on, and I love pressure. My biggest reason was that I am a person who completes tasks, and hopes to do well in them, if I'm passionate about it. By now my

personal development had got me well interested and stuck in."

The life coach relationships

Keith Horsfall's stark assessment is that the Ballet Hoo! life coach arrangements failed the young people. The coaches were recruited too late and there were too few of them. Some were possibly unsuitable. All the young people were assigned life coaches but some life coaches had to work with more than one young person. For one reason or another many did not develop their coaching relationships. Some young people made no effort to keep in touch or avoided their life coach some of whom, it would appear, then gave up trying to make the relationship work. One youth said:

"I was assigned a life coach. We only met once because I didn't feel comfortable. So I decided how far I could go on my own to see if I was

willing to help myself."

Four girls described their experience as follows:

"I started off really good with my life coach, meeting every two weeks. Then she left for like two months and I never had one. Then I had a new one, but I avoided meeting up with her."

"J was my life coach. We met once throughout the whole project. He told me his life story and then I didn't see him again."

'I had a life coach for about four days and then I never saw her again. She never kept in contact and didn't even show up at the performance.'

"Throughout the project I had two life coaches but only one of them contacted me. But I never got to meet him, so I never got to know him."

In other cases, however, the life coach relationship was powerfully supportive, as C's story makes clear. C was not alone in this respect:

"T was my life coach. I only saw her when I was at the project. But she supported me. Sitting down with her I achieved one of my life goals – I stopped smoking for five weeks. I started again, but I'm going to give up again. It's about confidence."

"My life coach was D who was very involved in my personal development process, as well as always encouraging me in the performance aspects. I met up with her quite often outside of sessions and she was a great help to me, as we grew closer and maintained friendship."

"The first life coach I had dropped out towards the end of the first phase. During that time I made friends with another life coach who took over afterwards. We met reasonably frequently and kept in touch. We got to know each other and we still make regular contact today, since the project ended."

"My life coach's name was S. She was a great woman. She gave me phone calls often and we met up once or twice. Because life coaching was getting in the way of her work she had to stop coming to the sessions. But she still came and watched my performance at the Hippodrome."

"I did have a life coach. She was very supportive and helped me out a lot. We didn't meet up that often, but that's mostly because I kept having things on. We did talk regularly though and emailed a lot. We still do. She became a close friend to me – just a more mature one – that really helped me."

Nor was it always necessary for young people to get close to their life coaches for the relationship to prove helpful. One girl recorded:

"I did have a life coach and her name was H. We never met often but when she was there she was always helpful. I feel we never knew each other very well but it didn't affect the support she gave me when she was around."

Moreover some relationships worked constructively despite initial or occasional tensions:

'I felt weird about it at first. But after meeting her I felt okay about it. But sometimes she would get in my way, like if I wanted to sit out for a while. She would push me until I did it. It was annoying sometimes. But I'm glad she did it now.'

When interviewed, C in her story, suggested that because the young people weren't able to choose their life coaches, many didn't bother contacting them. To begin with she thought she didn't need a life coach. But later, because her life coach persisted in a thoroughly professional manner, she came to appreciate the support and the relationship became a strong one.

Relationships with the Project Co-ordinators

The four project co-ordinators with the two seconded Connexions staff took the major role in managing the young people: making sure venues, transport and food were provided and offering endless support and encouragement. Taxis never seemed to be on time, food was always an issue and the young people in the early days needed a great deal of coaxing to get them out of bed and to the project!

When the life coach 'crisis' arose, the co-ordinators and Connexions staff stepped into the breach and acted as life coaches for many young people who were not otherwise being supported. They often acted as 'interpreters' for YAR when the young people did not understand the language or concepts used. They also acted as 'coaches' to the life coaches who sometimes struggled to understand the rejecting and challenging behaviour of the young people.

Their role demanded more than anyone could have expected at the start of the project and it is clear that without their dedication many of the young people's journeys would not have been so successful. A year after the project, Michelle Bould and Ali Reilly, who now work full time for Dudley- based Leaps & Bounds, and Denzil Peart who now works as a self-employed youth worker, were spoken of with affection by the Ballet Hoo! graduates, many of whom are still in regular contact with them. If lasting relationships are key to effective youth work, then the Ballet Hoo! project established them for a high proportion of the young people involved.

Phase Two and the Hippodrome Performance

'Brilliant'; 'mind blowing'; 'incredible'; 'overwhelming'; 'exhilarating'; 'magical'; 'amazing'; 'once-in-a-lifetime'; 'orgasmic'; 'the biggest buzz ever'; 'words can't describe it' – this is how the 62 young people who performed at the Hippodrome on 28 September 2006 described the event. Their enthusiasm was matched by the audience, many of whom, including Desmond Kelly and Marion Tait who trained them, cried with joy. It was for many of us one of the greatest evenings we have ever had in the theatre. For the young people it was the culmination of six months intensive, hard work. Phase Two began in April 2006 with a presentation from Desmond Kelly on what would be required of the young people. The focus was the rehearsal, preparation and staging of Romeo and Juliet. Everyone got a briefing pack that included timetables, roles and responsibilities, a contract of engagement, the expectations of BRB staff, fitness and warm-up exercises and a reminder of the project ground rules. The latter had been added to since Phase One. The new demands concerned

committing to and attending rehearsals and being prompt and prepared, whether this was for ballet or personal development work. The young people were told they would be respected and treated as a member of BRB.

The dance offer comprised the opportunity to perform, 'in character', the large crowd scenes such as the fight between the Montagues and Capulets; more demanding roles in group scenes such as the Mandolin dance; major individual roles such as Juliet's parents, Friar Lawrence and The Nurse. Casting took place in late April. Motivation was to some extent gender driven. Romeo and Juliet has better roles for men than women: there are more and better solo parts for them and their ensemble pieces include a fight scene, the 'Tun–Up' and the 'Mandolin dance'. The women have only the Ballroom and the Harlot scenes. The consequence was greater overall commitment and engagement from the young men. It was not until the costumes were fitted and make-up and hair styles discussed that the majority of the girls really engaged. There were exceptions to this pattern, but many of the girls appeared initially to use rehearsals disruptively as time for meeting up with friends.

In the summer, while BRB staff were taking their holiday, the young people were given the opportunity to attend a 40 hour fitness course at Aston Villa Football Club. Sixteen young people took advantage of this opportunity. There was a balance of health and fitness sessions covering stamina training, health education including diet, smoking, drug and alcohol information sessions and opportunities to work in a radio production studio. There were some unexpected results from this programme: five participants came off anti-depressants; six young people gave up smoking; three amended or curtailed their drinking habits; and others learned that sport and dance could be complementary.

Back at BRB there were frequent problems of young people not turning up for rehearsals or arriving late. This made it difficult for BRB to build the skill base for the ensemble pieces. It was agreed there would be a 'three strikes' rule, rigorously applied. Anyone not arriving for rehearsal would receive a strike. Three strikes and you left the project. This was difficult to police, the rule was applied unevenly and the young people thought it unfair. But it did drive home the importance of commitment and turning up on time. Attendance and punctuality improved. Nevertheless rehearsals were often chaotic and noisy. Desmond and Marion found themselves handling large groups of young people and life coaches some of whom were dancing and others not. Selected BRB dancers were brought in to assist.

Apart from attending the partners' kick-off workshop, neither Desmond Kelly nor Marion Tait underwent the YAR training, but they did sit at the back of some of the intensive YAR sessions for the young people. Desmond says he felt uncomfortable with it. He initially considered it exploitive, possibly sharing some of the reservations which led Stephen Ball from the Birmingham Rep to not take part. However, he now doubts the young people would have coped with the BRB programme without the YAR training. It removed some barriers. Further, Desmond confesses that having spent a lifetime in ballet he was changed by Ballet Hoo! The project made him more conscious of the influence of an individual learner's background on how they learn. He says he now feels

the need to know more about the personal lives and backgrounds of the young people he's teaching. As a result he is more comfortable in his job and feels he has more authority in it.

Desmond's admission is paralleled by the young people's perceptions of him. In the eyes of L, there were two Desmonds - that at the beginning of the project and that at the end.

"We changed them and they changed us: it couldn't have worked without the two sides coming together. To begin with he was just insisting on us getting it right. But when we did, he cried. We saw that he was human and that he cared. We saw that he was happy because we achieved."

Prejudices were also broken down. C records that Marion Tait, who she now regards as a friend, once told her that before Ballet

Hoo! she would probably have crossed the road to avoid some of the young people taking part. But like Desmond, Marion cried when she watched their collective achievement at the Birmingham Hippodrome. I know because I sat behind both of them in the theatre. I cried also, without at that stage having got to know a single one of them.

The personal development sessions ran back to back with the rehearsals. This created a dilemma for the life coaches whose own timetables sometimes clashed with that of the young person they were coaching. BRB were also unclear whether they wanted the life coaches to perform on stage. There were mixed views amongst the life coaches. Some felt that by performing they would be providing positive role models for the young people. Others felt that their role was to guide and

support the young people from the side during the performance. In the end the life coaches made their own choice whether to perform or not and all but one of the twelve who remained at the end of the project performed on stage. Fred Richings, who acted as a life coach as well as being project co-ordinator for Dudley, considers that in the early months of Phase Two the uncertainties surrounding the life coach role led to a degree of disillusionment amongst some of the life coaches and an increasing sense that they were being treated inconsiderately. He thinks this may explain why so many departed.

The final rehearsal push came two weeks before the performance. There was a noticeable change in the attitudes of the young people: they became more positive, concentration increased and there was a sense of them being one

company. In the last week this trend was even more marked. The first three television programmes were aired in the three weeks running up to the performance and for some of the young people this was the moment when they realised what they were engaged in.

The Channel 4 documentary series and the 'disadvantaged' label

Everyone involved watched the tv series. But in a surprising proportion of cases the young people's comments on it were grudging and in a few cases severely critical. The key issues, as the following quotes illustrate, were the characterisation of the group as 'under-privileged' or 'disadvantaged' and the focus on bad behaviour, both of which were regarded as a distortion.

"My family weren't happy with the label 'under-privileged.'"

"A bit out of order, because people will call us disadvantaged."

"I felt we were misinterpreted and portrayed in a very mistaken light. It made it seem as if we were all from the same background, which we weren't."
"It was a load of shit. I am not disadvantaged. They made it look bad."

"I feel it never showed everyone's life stories. They never showed the positive side to the experience and journey we went through. It gave us all a bad name and a label which I never used to have."

"I didn't like it very much. I don't think they showed the millions of viewers everything that really went on. They tried to make out that everyone was deprived and that after the project that we were all reformed or changed because of it. Which wasn't entirely true."

"I thought it was OK but they never shown anything good – parties, etc – just bad stuff – fights, etc."

"There were high and low points. High was seeing myself on TV. Low was the way we were talked about. The description of disadvantaged. That was

offensive. People say to me now, 'I never realised you were disadvantaged'."

Some, however, understood that focusing on the negatives had been an entertainment technique unavoidable with television:

"I thought that it was good in a way because it made the show more exciting and entertaining for the audience

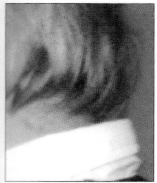

– but it made us seem bad."

"I thought it was entertaining. But there were too many negatives in it – the fighting and arguing."

There were inevitable reservations about the creation of 'stars':

"It was a little bit too focused on people with big problems. I was never interviewed, so I never got to hear my own voice. But I knew the people. I had been there. So I was fascinated."

"It wasn't how I thought they would do it. Most people that were on the project weren't even seen on the TV. They only focused on certain people, which I didn't find fair."

"Some were highlighted in the show more than others, I personally thought the documentary did not show our team effort, but focused instead on selected people. All should be equal."

The Ballet Hoo! staff anticipated all these issues and think that the Diverse Productions team fully earned the trust invested in them. They point to the multiple benefits that the TV series earned for everyone concerned: the prospect of the TV series attracted many of the young people to the project and helped to keep them with it; the positive publicity gained by the key organisations was beyond that which one could purchase; and several of the young people had undoubtedly had their personal career prospects greatly enhanced (see, in particular, the individual accounts of C, L and S). Diverse filmed throughout the project and it was inevitable that those young people who revealed or said

striking things during the initial YAR training sessions would be developed as characters and story lines – which meant that they had to the greatest possible extent to be kept in play and given the opportunity to shine in the final performance. The project co-ordinators and BRB staff to some extent colluded with the film production pressures and tactics, with respect to both selection and support, to ensure that outcome. But there is no suggestion that the manipulation was disproportionate or unethical and the fact is that the young people did achieve mastery and shine on the night.

Indeed the tv production process was arguably testimony to the proposition that given support and encouragement many young people are capable of achieving mastery.

Changed lives?

The Ballet Hoo! project was a relatively intensive, complex package with many ingredients: personal development training; the discipline of learning to dance; engagement in repeated teamwork exercises; making new friends from different geographical areas and cultural backgrounds; the support of life coaches and co-ordinators; and performing in front of expectant audiences. Absorbing all that represented a process of becoming. Thus, perhaps not surprisingly, the young people when asked whether Ballet Hoo! "changed their lives" (the sub-title of the tv series), tended to reject the 'life-changing' notion as inappropriate or simplistic: it wasn't like that. They emphasised that young people aged 15-18 are, after all, developing anyway. At 18 one is not the same as when one was 16, and the project lasted 18 months. And yet, for most of them, their home circumstances – their family relations, the neighbourhoods where they live, their intimate social networks, their cultural affiliations, their schools or colleges – remained largely the same. This tension between the changing and the unchanging character of their lives is apparent from their responses.

"It never changed my life. It just gave me an insight to what I am and what I'm capable of doing."

"Not changed my life as to make it better because I was and still am happy with my life. But it changed it in the sense that I don't know what else I would be doing."

"I think people get confused with the question of whether ballet changed them, or their life. Ballet did change my life because I spend so much time rehearsing. I found an interest in ballet. However, I don't think it changed my life. I would still be in the 6th form, and still have the same career in mind."

"No, not in many aspects. Just in the aspect that I have new things and ways in my life."

"No, I feel it has helped me manage it and organise it. I don't think it has changed my life – more that it has enhanced my understanding of my own life. Though I do feel that the BRB team has inspired me to have more confidence in myself."

"It didn't change my life. It made me think about different things going on in it. I did and now they are sorted."

"It opened my eyes to other people's issues. But I didn't feel as if it changed my life. It just made me look at things from a different point of view."

"I don't think the project has changed my life. But it has opened many doors in my life."

"The project changed my attitude, especially on myself. It raised my confidence, my self esteem. I'm not so shy. I can open up to others without holding back."

"It opened my eyes and introduced me to a wide range of different people and cultures. I respect people who are real and themselves."
"Yes, because I don't know if I necessarily thought it before but it made me realise that it takes work to make things happen."

"I feel that the project didn't change my life. But it improved my way of thinking and my perspective about the image that I and others present, I think that has now been changed and people are seeing us differently."

"It didn't change my life. That's too strong. But it made it better. Made me more confident, lively and sociable. I'm getting a JCB

job as a quarryman when I've got my JCB licence at college. I'll be earning £25 an hour."

Some took a thoughtful, long term view which hints at the difficulties faced by any formal evaluation of a project like Ballet Hoo!:

"I feel it did change my life, and everyone else's. You cannot experience something like that and not change in some way because of it. It changed my life in a lot of different ways, a lot of which I don't even know."

"Yes, I think it inspired me. It brought out my talents and made me part of something. Other than that it has on occasion changed me in ways I can't put my finger on."

As to what, exactly, it was about Ballet Hoo! that might have changed them, the young people set considerable store by the friendships they had developed:

"Building up of friendships has enabled me to speak openly about what I want to do with my future. I felt more reserved beforehand."

"Building friendships over time. Because my friendships mean everything to me.

And to meet new people who I know I care a lot for makes me a happier person."

"Contact with a variety of people that I don't encounter every day. Just seeing other people's issues. Coming to the project was great, interacting with other people because I was grounded for two years before it began." Finally, the young people stressed the importance of the front line staff – people like Desmond Kelly and Marion Tait from BRB, the key local authority project co-ordinators, Michelle Bould, and Denzil Peart and Ali Reilly from Black Country

Connexions – who, in a sense, were, in the minds of the young people, the embodiment of the lessons that the project sought to instil – discipline, choice, resolution, commitment, living with the consequences of one's actions, mutual respect. One youth summed it up in a manner which those staff will find gratifying:

"The discipline – time outs – this made me think more about what and how I wanted to be. To ask "Am I thinking the right way? Do I want to mess this opportunity up" Also, the coaching – that related to the way I am. They have to

have given thought to something to get the job of co-ordinator. The staff had to have gone through issues before – so they knew what I needed."

The Future

Without exception the Ballet Hoo graduates thought there should be further projects of a similar nature because, as one of them put it: "It's bettered me – it could help others."

There was no consensus regarding how future projects might or should be different; responses depended on individual experience. Some, for example, wanted more committed life coaches. Others wanted things to be more activity-based with less talking. Others, by contrast, considered the inclusion of the four-day personal development training to be vital. However, whatever form future projects take, almost everyone offered to help with the organisation of them. Ballet Hoo! had sown civil society seedlings, some with distinctly disciplinary inclinations:

"Yes, I'd help as a peer mentor, coach. Knuckle down. If they won't listen to co-ordinators, coaches, dancers or me – they will be sent home."

L's Story

I arranged to meet L at his mother's house in Netherton on the edge of Dudley. Here he lives with a younger brother and sister. The area looks as if it was originally a council estate but the houses are of a superior design and most have the appearance of having been bought and personalised by their occupants. Everything is very neat and well cared for.

When I parked my car in front of the house a small girl in school uniform with pigtails was standing at the front door ringing the bell. I got out and introduced myself. I asked if L lived there. She said he did, but probably wouldn't be home until about 5 o'clock, in two hours time. I said I hoped that wouldn't be the case because I'd arranged to meet him at three. I went and sat in the car. The small girl went off up the street. She proved to be L's sister. No one being at home she went to either her aunt or Gran, both of whom lived nearby.

Shortly thereafter L came home on foot. We sat in the small front room. The house is very small, but full of books and plants. The walls are covered with family photos and framed original pictures, several of them by L's second sister, who he explained had recently moved to London. While we talked both L's mother and younger brother came home. I had brief chats with both of them. They were welcoming and extremely articulate, but left us in the front room to carry on our talk in private. When the time came for me to go I chatted with L's mother for five minutes while L Google-mapped the address of my next interview. She told me a few things that L had shielded from me. Despite there being some tensions between them, L is clearly protective of his mother. I'm 17 and I've lived in this house with my mother and brother and sisters for about five years. Before that we moved about quite a lot. I was born in Croydon, South West London. My Dad still lives there. He has two older sons, my half brothers. I can't say when exactly my Mum and Dad split up because their relationship was so on-off when I was younger. We, my Mum and my brother and two sisters, moved up here where my Mum's family come from, and then we moved backed to Croydon, and then back here again. Relations between my Mum and Dad are quite friendly now, but when I was young it was pretty hectic. [At this point L's Mum comes home, but soon retires to the kitchen to leave us alone] My Dad's family originally came from Jamaica, as did my Mum's Dad. I was taken to Jamaica when I was about four, but I don't remember much about the visit. We have a video of the visit, and most of what I remember is from the video. I don't think anyone's been back since.

I spent most of my primary school years in London, but most of my secondary in the Midlands. In Year 5, I moved to the Midlands and went to two more primary schools up there during Year 6. We ended up living in a mixture of hostels, family member's houses and our own before moving back to London to my previous school and house before my Year 6 SATS. Because we moved back to London at a time when everyone had been allocated to their schools of choice, I ended up going to one of the roughest, lowest achieving schools in the area. Because the school was so under-achieving and dangerous, my parents were able to get me into a better school not too far away. Although the school terms had started, I think my SATS grades were reason enough for me to be accepted. A year later, we ended up moving back to the Midlands to my third and last secondary school, meaning that altogether I've been to three primary schools, three secondary schools and one sixth form college, which is why I have to write on the back of application forms when explaining where I've been educated.

On the whole school has been a pretty good experience for me. Moving about between schools, which I did a lot, can be unsettling. But I think it was lucky for me. I think I benefited. I was quite introverted when I was younger. But I think that as result of moving about so much I gained a better understanding of people and gained the ability to learn fast. The first secondary school I went to in Croydon, Stanley Tech, was hopeless. There were fights on the playground all the time, the kids weren't learning and the teachers couldn't teach. I was a weakling when I was smaller, so there was no way I could contend with all of that. My parents knew they had to get me out of there, so they got me into another school. My Mum asked me when it came to moving to the Midlands: "Shall we, as a family, move for good up to Dudley?" Because of the general situation at home I said "Yes". My parents had split up. We were all living in the same house, but my Mum had moved downstairs into the dining room and put a lock on the door. There were arguments in the house every day. You couldn't get a word in. When I tried to calm things down and said stop, stop, stop, they used to turn on me and then the argument would be about me. It was pretty unpleasant and I found it fairly traumatic. So I said yes, let's move, even though it meant leaving a lot of friends, some of

whom I still keep in touch with. It was my decision, a pretty big decision, that we move, but we needed to settle down. I still look back on that decision and regret it sometimes because of what I had to leave behind. It makes me wonder what things would be like now if I'd decided we should stay down there.

Moving meant I was given a second chance. It meant that if things didn't go too well, I was given a fresh chance with each move. By the time I got to my long-term secondary school up here I knew how to be top of the class. I knew how to be a popular kid without having to be a naughty kid, which is what I saw a lot of other kids doing. And I knew how to

get out of trouble. I was popular in school when I came up here partly because I was from London and I had a cool accent. But whatever the case I got along with everyone.

I went to Hillcrest School in Dudley. It's a pretty big school, but not as big as the one in London, and it's over-subscribed. It's quite hard to get into, but it doesn't have a sixth form. I'm not sure how it was in comparison to my previous school, but it was calmer, more peaceful, more relaxed, than the school in London. It was pretty strict. If you were out of line, you were definitely out of line. But you could have fun with the education there. Of course there were occasional fights, but after

seeing the ones in Stanley Tech, I wouldn't class them as fights at all. It was completely different from Croydon.

Racism? I've never really come across it. In London it wasn't an issue because anyone who behaved in a racist way would have been racist to half the class. And I've never experienced racism or discrimination up here even though the racial minorities really are minorities here. We're not discriminated against or if we are I haven't noticed it. Up here most of my friends are white because most people are white. In my sixth form college there are only four of five black guys in my whole year in a college of 663. You get reactions

sometimes. For example, I've got a friend who's lighter skinned than me but he wears American-style very hip-hop clothes – baggy pants and so on. And I remember the first time he came into the large hall at college, the whole hall fell silent. It's a very English, middle class place where, to begin with, I felt slightly uncomfortable. Because I'd never had contact before with such a middle class place. I know I'm English, but I'm not the same kind of English. And I'm not Jamaican. So what am I? I don't know. I'm not a Brummie, I'm not a Yam Yam and I'm not a London Cockney either. But I feel comfortable with who I am.

I was always academic. Really good at English. Really good at maths. Pretty good at science, though I didn't much like science. I wasn't into sports. I had drama classes outside school between seven and nine, but it didn't really work magic for me back then. It was year eight or nine that I was properly introduced to drama. I remember we were

doing some play in class. I was just doing it without thinking much about it. And I remember the teacher saying to me "You really can act. You're a really good actor. You should audition for the school show." I hadn't thought about drama. It seemed easy. You just did it. But I did go for the school show after that. And I was in it. Then the same next year. And the year after that. It became part of what I did. I wasn't thinking, this is good or bad or I'm good at it or I'm bad at it. It was just there, and I did it.

Even so I felt life was patchy. School was usually alright. But once I stepped through the door at home things were a bit fractious. In the holidays I often went to Croydon, and I got on really well with my older half brothers. But we had a lot of problems. There is no way that I can say that my family is happy, at all. No way.

My Mum has a compressed disc and arthritis and is in pain constantly. She gets really stressed out from it. She has to take a lot of painkillers and the painkillers turn her into a completely different person. It's unbelievable. Her reactions become very negative and because of that there is a really negative influence on the family. So there are often tensions.

I got to hear about the Ballet Hoo project through my school Head of Drama. Fred and Ali [Fred Richings and Ali Reilly, respectively co-ordinator for Dudley and Black Country Connexions] asked her to identify suitable students for the project. She got all the people she thought were suitable together and asked us if we were interested. She told us it was for 'disadvantaged' kids and when those of us who were interested asked what should we put on the form, she suggested "Say your Mum smokes, or something like that." So, that's what I put. And I got in. My drama teacher didn't know anything else about

my personal circumstances which she could have told Ali or Fred. I think her motivation was simply that a project like Ballet Hoo, with the opportunity of working with Birmingham Royal Ballet and getting on tv, would be a great opportunity for us. Simply that. And it was a great opportunity.

About 10 or 12 kids from Hillcrest School were enrolled for Ballet Hoo. A couple of them left on the first day of the four day intensive training – they didn't even make it through the day. They didn't like it. And then another half dozen or so didn't come back for the second or third day. So, when the programme started proper there were only about four of us left. One girl walked out during the first break on the first morning of the first day. I think they should have started with an overview about what the project as a whole was going to be like. Because those who left on the first day would not have known how the project was going to end up. I think people dropped out right at

the beginning because it was too much like school: a lot of sitting down and a lot of talking. They mostly didn't continue not because of the ground rules but simply because they were bored.

I didn't have a problem with the ground rules. I think most of the problems that arose about them were because of the way in which the rules were enforced – like, if you kept your hat on there was a whole big fuss. Like the American woman, Denise, who was the group leader was on to you straight away for the smallest thing. Like you only had to ask the person sitting next to you what the time was in a low voice and Denise was straight away pointing at you and going 'Sssshhhhhhh!'

Even so I could understand why they had the ground rules. They needed to be there. The ground rules kept everyone on the same level and everyone knew where they were. The problem was that people signed the ground rules contract without appreciating what they were signing.
The thing I learned most from the initial intensive training was about the others in the group. Because if you just looked at them

you didn't know where they were coming from, what they'd been through, that sort of thing. I learned that other people had been through similar things that I'd been through. Things like moving about from place to place: when I heard someone describe that I thought, just like me. I would never have found out about that otherwise. You don't learn about that sort of stuff in school. You've no idea at school about what's going on in other people's lives. And within the project we went on learning about each other. Right at the end, after 18 months, I was still learning about things that I had no idea about and would never have suspected. That was valuable. At school it's all just about getting grades, passing exams and so on. The good thing about the project, and the initial training, was that we learned that we're not alone with whatever we're going through. That was important for bettering people's lives. It meant that we knew about the issues we had to address.

It may also have been important for making us into a team. I'm not sure about this. You see, at the

beginning there were about 200 of us, and 200 can never be a team It's too daunting. Too many people with too many different smaller groups. But when the numbers got down a bit, we ended up bonding as a group, which was important. We ended up doing better than anyone thought we would. For me, the personal development stuff – having the friendships – got me to the place where I could do the major role of Tybult in the final production sooner than I think I could otherwise have done. I think I could have done it without the personal development – but it would have taken me longer. I felt secure with the others and I had greater confidence to do it.

If you're asked quickly to think back about the intensive personal development training, I think one tends to say it was rubbish and boring – simply because there was so much sitting about, and listening and talking. But if you delve into it, there was quite a lot going on that was important.

I did my GCSEs in the middle of the second phase of Ballet Hoo, when we preparing for the performance in 2006. I got seven As, three Bs, a C and a D – 12 altogether. I got Bs in maths and English literature. How would I have done in my GCSEs without the project? I'm not sure. The rehearsals didn't really start to get intensive until after I'd taken my GCSEs. But I'd already changed as a person. I had become much less academic and much more performing arts oriented. I was becoming less keen on sitting down and doing academic work – and in that sense I might have done better in my exams if I hadn't done the Ballet Hoo project.

I'm doing three A Levels now, ICT, Drama and English. I was doing four, but I've just dropped Psychology. I just can't take too much sitting down, listening and learning facts any more. And I'm doing a lot of other things. I'm in practically every drama production at college, King Edwards VI - it's one of the best sixth form colleges in the country. I'm working with Connexions as a Dudley Young Advisor: we go to conferences, hold meetings and workshops for young people. And we consult with various agencies about how to get young people more involved and engaged. I get

paid for doing that. I've also got a part in a local theatre production of Mice and Men at the Netherton Arts Centre. It's the first part I've got in a proper theatre production outside school or college or Ballet Hoo. My role is prominent, but it's not a major role. We'll be doing three performances in March 2008. And then I did a National Youth Theatre performance in the summer holidays. I'm out most evenings and at weekends.

After my A Levels I want to have a gap year and travel a bit. Then I want to go to drama school. I don't want to go to university because I'm sick of studying. I don't want to do a drama course, I want to do drama. Why would I want to write about it, when I can do it? I was going to apply now, but I'd rather do it after I've travelled a bit.

My Mum's very proud of me, but it doesn't come across. There's a lot frustration at home because I'm out so much and I'm not helping much at home. When I am home I'm again not helping because I've got my A Level work to do. My Mum doesn't have a job, but she's doing a part-time college course.

I've become quite prominent locally because of the Ballet Hoo project. In fact the local paper seems always to find an excuse to put me in the paper. I was in it the other day because I'd presented a youth award. I don't think there's been a downside to all the publicity, though there would be if I got into any trouble, which I don't intend to do. I wasn't aware that there were jealousies within the Ballet Hoo project about me getting the big part, until I later heard that X had wanted the part of Tybult and was a bit pissed off that he hadn't got it. And then Y was taking part in the National Youth Theatre show that I was involved this summer and people told me that he literally hated me because he said I was getting all the best parts. That shocked me. Indeed, I couldn't believe it. I think I got the big part in Ballet Hoo because I deserved it. I worked hard for it.

The Hippodrome performance was fantastic. I wasn't nervous until the night before. Even when we were in the changing rooms, half an hour before the show, we were still doing a fun rap competition. But then when we came to the stage, just before the curtain

went up, I was suddenly so scared. I had to lead the rest of the group, including BRB members, on. When I saw the audience, I thought wow. We'd done a rehearsal on that stage before, but there was virtually no one in the seats. And now there were 2000 people. But after about ten minutes, it just seemed natural to be there. In the third act my group didn't have much to do. I was lying down on the tomb backstage, ready to be wheeled on for the final scene, and several of the cast were around me having the most beautiful, peaceful conversation. X was there, C, the backstage manager was there, Courtney was there, and a few others. We had to whisper because the show was still going on, but that only made the moment more special. It was then that we all came to the realisation that, 'This is the last time we'll ever be together like this', and it was.

I made lots of friends in the project. Denzil [Denzil Peart, the Birmingham Co-ordinator] in particular amongst the staff, though he was more like one of us: he was with us all the other time, dancing with us and everything. And Ali [Ali Reilly, the Black Country Connexions Co-ordinator]. She was amazing: everyone loved Ali. Then there was a guy called Donald, who helped us in the early days of the project with Sunday dance workshops. And Desmond [Desmond Kelly, the Artistic Director] of course. I loved Desmond. With Desmond, it was weird. During the first part of the project there was one Desmond, who you really couldn't connect with. He

was Birmingham Royal Ballet. Very formal. But in summer 2006, when we got into the intensive rehearsals, he seemed to take more interest in us. He was almost less professional about it all. I won't say it was calm, because it could be hectic at times. But he was a different Desmond: more human. I've kept in touch with him since. In fact I spoke to him the other day about drama school: he's going to speak to someone for me.

Ballet Hoo is definitely the best thing I've done so far - the high point in my life. It's made me more ambitious. It's changed me in that respect. I have greater expectations and I believe now that I can tackle things. When Desmond first showed me what Tybalt had to do in Romeo and Juliet I thought, 'no, no, no, no - there's no way I can do that'. But I didn't tell him that, because if I did I knew I wouldn't get

the part. But I got the part and after learning the role, I thought, 'I could do it after all. Good thing I never told anybody my doubts about it'. Now, regardless of whether or not I think I can, I try and tackle everything that comes my way. And the majority of the time I manage things. If someone were to offer me the part of the next James Bond, I'd instantly think that there's no way I could do it. But I wouldn't openly say that. I'd go for it

and make sure that I could. Before the Ballet Hoo project I would probably have said, no, I don't think I should attempt it. Now it's different. Next steps for me are the Mice and Men production and then A Levels and then I hope some travel during a gap year. My family is really high achieving. My oldest half brother works in the marketing division of EA, the biggest games company in the world, he's a fantastic communicator. My oldest sister, who's just moved to London, is an amazing artist. My Mum is very creative and makes the most amazing decorated cakes: no one can make cakes like her. It's clear my sister got her artistic talents from her, and my mum's cooking puts every restaurant to shame. I've got a lot to live up to in terms of achievement. I want an artistic career now. If I don't 'make it', then I don't. I am realistic. I know it may not happen. I still have a sense of proportion. But I'm going for it.

While waiting for L to produce on his computer a map for my next appointment I chatted with his Mum in the kitchen. She was making the most astonishing, intricate, sugar decorations for a cake. Extraordinarily skilled work. Without any prompting she told me much more than L had told me about his disrupted early life, about the breakdown of her longstanding relationship with his father and the very serious consequences of another relationship she had had, all of which would likely have had adverse consequences for L's development and emotional stability. In which case he has done brilliantly well and, despite everything, L's Mum is clearly very proud of his achievements.

chapter 7

'what a result'

To the ad hoc comments of the young people we can add more systematic evidence about outcomes, evidence of the sort which any tough-minded decision maker or funder is likely to want provided.

Exit interviews were undertaken with the Phase Two graduates and summary data supplied for an independent evaluation report.

Seventy per cent of the young people involved considered they had achieved the life goals they set for themselves at the start of the project. The most commonly selected life goals were health-related and the young people reported loss of weight, improved fitness, reduced or ceased smoking, etc. This is subjective self-appraisal, there being no clinical assessment of their health (obesity, fitness, and so on).

Analyses of the situation of the 42 Dudley, Sandwell and Wolverhampton young people at the end of 2006 showed:

- greatly improved engagement in education, training and employment (of nine NEETs in spring 2005, there was only one in late 2006);
- of the ten young people who were 'looked after' there continued to be a good deal of accommodation instability. None stayed at the same address throughout the project, two of them moving no fewer than eight times, if hotels and B&Bs are included;
- half the smokers no longer smoked and the majority of the remainder now had a reduced habit;
- of six young people with alcohol problems at the start, only one still had that problem at the close;
- everyone reported an improvement in their general health and fitness;
- four fifths had improved relationships with their parents or carers;

- only one young person felt that their peer relationship had not improved by the close of the project;
- none reported further incidents of self-harm or dependence on anti-depressants; of 18 young people who reported mental health problems at the time of enrolment only two had problems which had not lessened or been resolved at the end (but one was a long term bulimic and had agreed to counselling for the first time)
- only two criminal offences were recorded against members of the cohort since the start of the project, one during the project and one since;
- of 18 young people who admitted to having problems controlling their anger at the outset only one felt that remained the case at the close;
- everyone reported improvements in their self-confidence.

Getting a recognised award had always been part of the initial project plan. Birmingham City Council was particularly keen that each of the young people should take part in the Arts Council-funded Arts Awards and the Sandwell and Dudley project co-ordinators trained as assessors. However, because previous work could not be accredited these awards proved not to be possible. In retrospect the young people should have been entered for these awards at the outset of Phase One. Nevertheless Sandwell College supported the re-writing of a Performing Arts BTEC to accommodate Phase Two of the project.

Most of the work for this was undertaken by Michelle Bould with BRB providing considerable support for the work programme. It means that most of the Ballet Hoo! graduates gained a paper qualification from the exercise.

The young people who graduated from Ballet Hoo! are a minority of the young people who enrolled. The project team are, however, insistent that it would be wrong to think of all those who did not graduate from Phase Two as having 'dropped out' or failed.

The Black Country project co-ordinators admit that at the time of enrolment they had limited knowledge about which young people would truly be suitable for the project and having taken their details they never saw or had contact with some of them again. They were not termed 'at risk' for nothing! Some said they wanted to participate but didn't mean it. Some were leading chaotic, unstable lives. Phone numbers proved to be wrong or unobtainable. Addresses proved to be no longer applicable. A few parents failed to give their consent. Some young people just disappeared.

Nevertheless, Michelle Bould, Ali Reilly and Keith Horsfall are still in touch with many of the young people who did not graduate from Phase Two. They point out that some decided, following the YAR four-day intensive training sessions, that their personal development could best be achieved through engagement in activities other than the Ballet Hoo! project. Others, particularly at the end of Phase One, felt that the demands the project would make on them would be incompatible with other commitments – family, education or work, sport and so on – which they rightly wanted to keep.

The project team are convinced, on the basis of subsequent contact, that each stage in the Ballet Hoo! process, including

enrolment, carried benefits for the young people. Where the enrolment was done as planned, it involved an independent adult not in an authority relationship with the young people, helping them with and listening to their self–analysis. This meant that, possibly for the first time, many of the young people were considering their life style, self-image and relationships in the round. Unlike their youth offending team supervisors, or their care team support workers, the Ballet Hoo! co-ordinators and trailblazers were not focused on the young person's offending behaviour or their relationships with foster parents; they were trying to encourage them to consider how they saw themselves as a whole.

Thus, the Leaps & Bounds team argue, it is incorrect to judge the success of Ballet Hoo! purely in terms of graduate outcomes. Further support for their view is to be found in the fact that some of the non-graduates from the Ballet Hoo! project have enrolled for the follow-on projects that Leaps & Bounds are now organising.

The success of Ballet Hoo is also more subtle than dry statistics and dramatic stories can attest. Fred Richings, the project co-ordinator for Dudley, illustrates the point. He talks about one Dudley youth, a graduate from the Hippodrome performance, who he recently invited to do a presentation at a local civic occasion (several Ballet Hoo! graduates, including this youth, have repeatedly undertaken this role). The young man declined. "No" he said "I've agreed I'm not going to do too much. I'm going to keep my life simple and concentrate on the things I have to do." Fred was impressed. The young man is engaged on a training scheme. This was precisely the exercise of rational, resolved choice which the YAR training sought to inculcate. A small, individual example, but a telling one.

The impact of the project is evident in the transformation of behaviour and attitudes of the young people. Lee and Michelle, the husband and wife team who provided the catering for the young people, bear testimony to this change. At the beginning Michelle admits to having been shocked by the rudeness and abuse that many of the young people gave them - "I'm not eating that fucking rubbish. I'm going to the take-out over the road." She describes many of them as "no hopers heading for a lifetime on the SS". Yet by the halfway point

in the project she says they had become "Lovely. The difference in them was amazing. They would offer to help carry the equipment, wrap up the food or clear away. It's lovely to meet them now, and they all seem to be so successful." Unsolicited observations of this sort often tell one more than a wealth of dry statistics. Put simply, the kids had become decent human beings, giving and earning respect.

One of the more unforeseen outcomes of the project was the powerful sense of community, belonging and family that the young people and staff increasingly felt over the 18 months. Along with the individual relationships the young people formed with each other and the staff, they also developed a relationship with the project itself. It was this that kept them coming back week after week; a sense of being part of and investing in something that was so far outside their previous experiences, and of such interest to so many people.

Andy's Story

Andy lives in a ground floor flat, paid for by social services, in a small terrace house in a side street just off the main dual carriageway through Dudley. The street is down-at-heel. Most of the residents in the street are of Asian origin. Andy has a kitchen, living room and bedroom. His living room has a TV and good collection of electronic equipment, including a PC with internet access. Andy was wearing a black Manchester United football shirt and when I arrived two young friends were with him. They went into the kitchen at the back so that Andy and I could talk alone..

I'm 20 and am working part-time as a youth service volunteer and trainee mentor. During the school holidays I've been working mostly during the days, but when the kids go back to school it'll be more in the evenings. I don't get paid. But in a few weeks I'm going to start a twelve week Princes Trust course after which I hope to get a job in retail, which I can combine with continuing to work as a youth service volunteer.

I've lived all my life in the Black Country. I was born in Wordsley just north of Stourbridge and spent my early years nearby in Brierley Hill. I was one of four brothers but one of them died when I was eight. For reasons that I don't want to discuss I was taken into care shortly afterwards. My family wouldn't be happy if I talked about why that happened and it became public knowledge. I was fostered first by my aunt. But that didn't really work out and I wasn't really able to settle down there. My aunt had two older girls and I was used to living in a home with boys. I wasn't happy and started playing up. Over the next few years I lived with two other foster parents, the second of whom I stayed with for several years in West Bromwich. I was with these last foster parents from the age of 10 until I was 16 and left school. They became like a second family to me and we keep in touch still. I didn't call them Mum and Dad – I called them by their names – and we had disagreements when I was growing up. But I came to respect them. When I got to them I met my match. They were experienced foster parents and had had to handle difficult tearaways before, so they knew what to do. They weren't going to back down from anything. They were very strict and I realised that I wasn't going to get away with anything. So I had to knuckle down.

I first started getting into trouble at junior school. I was always getting into fights, being rude to teachers and being sent home. I'm not sure why, though I may have been following my brothers in a way. They had got into trouble and one had been sent to a childrens' home. I wanted to be one of the lads. I don't remember the teachers putting a particular label on me. I don't think I ever had a diagnosis like ADHD or 'learning dfficulties'. But I was considered disruptive and got very behind in my school work. This continued into secondary school. I was expelled from two schools. After the first I went to an inclusion unit, a sort of sin bin, for a half a day a week for several months and when I was 14 I went a whole year without going to any school. School work was sent to my home and my foster parents made sure I did it. They made me work as if I was in school all day. They made me get up in the morning as if I was going to school and continue with my school work until about half past four in the afternoon. Then I got back into school and after another period of bother I decided that I liked the new school and realised that I didn't have much time left now. I came to my senses and settled down. I had a learning support teacher. I left school after taking my GCSEs. I got mostly Es and Fs but I passed Design Technology, or Manufacturing, with the equivalent of two GCSEs grade C.

I left home, my foster parents, when I was 16 and lived in a supervised hostel for young people. It was good. I got my own space and could do my own thing. There were four or five of us. It was all arranged and paid for by the 16 Plus social services team.

I started a painting and decorating course with a Sandwell New Horizons

training provider. But I kept failing the wallpapering assessment part of the work and I fell out with the training manager. He wasn't nice to me and I lost my rag and told him he could stick his course where the sun never shines. I quit the painting and decorating course. But then I had moved into my own flat and I didn't have a job and I got into a bit of a downward spiral. I wasn't doing anything. I found it difficult to get up and motivate myself. I didn't get into any real trouble – though I did get a final warning from the police for breaking a window when I was drunk one night – and I wasn't into drink or drugs: I didn't have any money for that. But my life wasn't going anywhere. And then one day my Connexions worker said "How would like to be on Channel 4?" – he didn't say anything about the personal development aspect - and I was referred to Leaps & Bounds. I had no idea what was involved, but I thought 'What the heck, I'm not doing anything': it was at least something for me to do.

I was interviewed by my Connexions worker. I can't remember much about the interview but he asked me to identify three goals for myself and I said: lose weight; stop smoking; and gain employment.

The four-day intensive experience at the beginning of the project was crap. Rubbish. It was all boring talk and very repetitive. I wasn't bothered about the personal development stuff and a lot of it was completely over my head: I didn't know what they were on about. But though I say it was crap I think it did help people to see themselves as others see them. I think it made us think about why we do the things we do. For myself, I thought I had it bad, but I began to see that others had it worse. I think that made us identify more with each other and become a team. I remember E. from Sandwell, for example, described in front of everyone what it was like to be 16 and having to bring up a baby as a young single mother. I went up to her afterwards and told her that I thought what she was doing was great. When it came to my turn I talked about how little was happening in my life, how I'd messed up with

the painting and decorating course and how I wanted to be a somebody rather than a nobody. They filmed that and what I said was repeated several times in the tv series. I don't know whether that affected the decision to give me the part of the friar in the Hippodrome performance. But I didn't talk about my family and why I was taken into care. I wouldn't have liked that to be filmed and broadcast. I know it would have made my family unhappy. In any case I didn't think it was relevant. It was my life and it was in the past, nothing to do with anyone else.

I think in the end it was a good thing that they made us stand up and talk about some things going on in our lives. Because if we hadn't done it no one would have known and then later someone might have said something without realising and upset someone, and everything could've been blown apart.

My mother died unexpectedly in August 2006. To this day I don't really know what happened and why she died. But it was a shock and I didn't go to the rehearsal that day. Though I had been in care and fostered since the age of eight I had always kept in touch with my Mum and Dad and seen them regularly. Until the age of 13 I had regular supervised visits with them, and afterwards I kept in touch myself. So when my Mum died I phoned Ali and said I wasn't coming in and my first thought was that I didn't want to go on. But then I thought: 'I can't jack it in'. Mum had been so excited that I was going to be in the show that it would have almost been to let her down had I not gone on. I knew I had to do it and I had to make something of my life.

I know now that Desmond and Marion at BRB had already decided to ask me to play the part of the friar.

But I didn't know that at the time and I think they thought that I might leave the project because of my mother's death. But I didn't. I came to rehearsal the following day and they offered me the part.

Unfortunately no one in my family came to the Hippodrome performance, but they saw it on the TV afterwards. I wasn't able to get in touch with my aunt to let her know, my Dad has had Parkinson's for many years and I couldn't arrange for him to be brought, and my two brothers were still too upset about my mother's death. I was so nervous on the night that I was cacking myself. The lights were so bright I couldn't see the audience. But somehow I did it. I kept telling myself: 'don't mess up'. I wanted to do it in memory of mother.

The TV series was good. But I didn't like that they called us all disadvantaged, because lots of the young people weren't disadvantaged at all and wanted to be involved just so that they could learn to dance better. And the series to some extent gave the impression that we were all getting into serious trouble – which we weren't.

The project has really helped me. I think I would have ended up in a young offenders institution if it hadn't been for the project. I think I would have slid further and further downhill, because I didn't have anything going on in my life at the time. But as a result of the project I've got much more self-confidence and motivation. I know better how to sell myself now. Further, Ali and Paul Wilkinson got me into the Pathfinders Mentoring scheme – which I've been doing for more than a year

now, and when I've done the Princes Trust programme that, together with completing the Leaps & Bounds, will look really good on my CV.

I'm optimistic about the future. I've passed Levels 1 and 2 youth work qualifications, though I've got to do part of it again because I've lost a folder with my portfolio of project work. I know I won't become a paid, professional youth worker because to do that I would have to get higher qualifications, go to university and that. I couldn't manage that. But I think I'll be able to combine voluntary youth work with some other employment. I'd like to get a job in retail. If I stick to that I hope eventually to get promotion and become a supervisor and then a manager. I want to continue youth work because I want to help others. People helped me when I got into trouble at school – my foster

parents, the learning support teacher, the 16 Plus team, The Leaps & Bounds team, and so on. I would like to do the same.

The Manchester United football shirt? I wear it and support them in memory of my brother who died. He was a Man U supporter. I know it's not my local team and I've been to see them only once. I went up to Old Trafford to see them play West Bromwich Albion. I was sat at the WBA supporters' end with WBA supporters. When Man U scored I forgot who I was with and jumped up and cheered. I saw everyone around me looking at me and I wondered how I was going to get out alive. It was like being a traitor. But that's why I wear the shirt. For my brother who died.

Shortly after this meeting with Andy I was talking to one of the Leaps & Bounds workers in their office in

Dudley. Andy's name came up. He'd been invited to take part in some celebratory event where prizes were being given out. But he declined to come. His reason was that he thought he should concentrate for the time being on his Prince's Trust course and the opportunities he hoped would arise from that. Andy is focused.

chapter 8

'leaps & bounds – what next'
Back to the Ground

If the Black Country has a heart, it is arguably Wren's Nest Hill, Dudley. It's an iconic site, geologically renowned for its fossils, and since 1956 a national nature reserve, the first geological nature reserve in the country.

The name, Wren's Nest, derives not from the bird but the Anglo-Saxon wrosne, meaning the link. It is possible that the name was applied to the site because the hill defines the boundary between the Severn and Trent watersheds. It links east and west and under it lies the Dudley Canal tunnel. It was on this limestone hill that Abraham Darby, the inventor of coke iron smelting and father of the industrial revolution, was born. For centuries limestone was quarried from within the hill, first as building material, then as an agricultural fertiliser and finally as blast furnace flux for the Black Country's iron and steel industry. The result is a series of vast caverns some going down one hundred metres to underground canal basins constructed to transport the extracted rock. As I write, in October 2007, Wren's Nest Hill is at the centre of attempts to secure national funding for a plan to open up the caverns and canals inside the hill.

Less well publicised is the Wrosne Project, which aims to link, and reconcile two post-War council estates, the Wren's Nest and Priory Estates, which sit on two sides of the hill. This project is the most immediately obvious part of the Ballet Hoo! legacy.

September 2006: the aftermath

September 28th 2006 was exhilarating for everyone involved in Ballet Hoo! The Hippodrome performance of Prokofiev's Romeo and Juliet had by any standard been a stunning success. But as Lady MacMillan, the choreographer Kenneth MacMillan's widow, warned in a moving speech from the triumphal stage after the performance, there was bound to be a come down.

For many of the participants the project had been at the centre of their lives for months. The question after this climactic high was: now what? The Dudley-based project team felt much the same way. For the past 18 months they had lived a frenetic existence, living, eating and dreaming the project. Normal family lives had been put on hold. There had been little or no time to reflect on what they were doing. So, in the days and weeks after 28th September they had to face up to two issues. First, what support could they now offer to the young people post project as no official exit strategy had been agreed. Secondly, what exactly had they learned from the project?

These questions were most critical for the Project Director, Keith Horsfall, who, ironically, had scarcely figured in the tv series. The other key project players - the BRB, YAR and Diverse Productions staff teams - were going back to their normal lives and programmes: their involvement was for most practical purposes over. As for the local authority staff, Denzil Peart, the Birmingham co-ordinator left the employ of Birmingham, Fred Richings and Ian Wright, the co-ordinators for Dudley and Wolverhampton respectively went back to their old jobs, and it seemed likely that Michelle Bould, the Sandwell coordinator and Ali Reilly from Black Country Connexions, would do the same. But Keith Horsfall knew that he didn't want to go back to what he'd been doing before, working as a community arts organiser. He felt he'd grown as a person. He was also inspired. He knew he'd been involved in something that had really made a difference to individual young people. He believed, though he'd not yet defined precisely what it was that he believed. But he'd latched on to a method which he wanted to attach to some sort of continuing structure.

Keith got encouragement from Andrew Sparke and from Dudley's Director of Children's Services, John Freeman. John observed that so many projects like Ballet Hoo! were one-offs: subsequent generations of young people didn't get the same opportunity. Couldn't something be done to embed and repeat the exercise? What about setting up a more-or-less-autonomous trust to continue the work which Ballet Hoo! had started?

This is what has been done.

Intereted partners have set up the Leaps & Bounds Trust, a company limited by guarantee, with an application to become a registered charity pending. The project has its offices alongside Black Country Connexions in the delightful canal-side Red Brick Cone complex on the Wolverhampton side of Stourbridge, an old glass foundry which is now a regional tourist attraction. In the office, alongside Keith, are Fred Richings, Michelle Bould, now employed by Dudley Council and Ali Reilly, still employed by Connexions but all now working full-time for the Trust, organising second-wave projects of a similar nature to Ballet Hoo!. At the time of writing two major projects are in train – the Wrosne Project, and a new musical, 'Chasing Fate'

whose title has been chosen by a combination of the artistic staff and the young people themselves. Before describing these projects we should first outline what the Leaps & Bounds team conclude they learnt from Ballet Hoo! and what ingredients they consider essential in future projects. What follows is the distillation of Keith, Michelle and Ali's collective thinking subsequent to 28 September 2006:

- The task is to reach disadvantaged young people at risk of which, regrettably, there are all too many within their immediate vicinity. The Leaps & Bounds constitution speaks of targeting young people with the greatest needs.
- Whatever practical or artistic skills training is offered to the young people, the activity will be integrated with personal development training. Projects currently being planned once again involve a partnership with YAR.
- The young people will also have the possibility of acquiring BTEC type qualifications such that they are able to leave projects with some form of accredited testimony to enhance their employability.
- Each young person will have life coach support. The life coaches will be recruited and trained prior to the enrolment of project participants so that they can be matched to and working with the young people from the outset.
- There will be established at the outset of each project a youth forum to represent the views of the young participants.

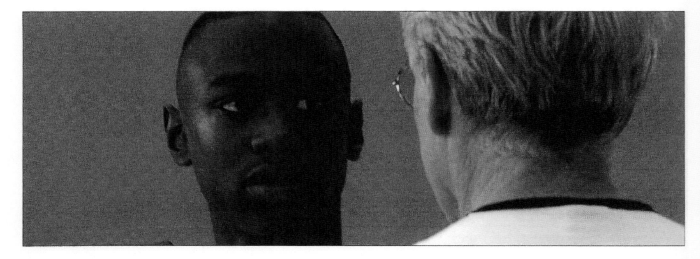

- Every project will have a built in exit strategy to support project graduates for a period after the training and performance (if applicable) has taken place.
- Systematic record keeping of participants' engagement will be maintained throughout each project and evaluation of outcomes will be integral to the administration of each. Finally, every project will be planned on the basis of a clear statement of desired outcomes.

Many of these stipulations arise from lessons learned, some the hard way, during the course of Ballet Hoo!. Take the last, for example. Because the Ballet Hoo! contract never defined precisely who the participating young people

should be, different local authorities were able to enrol candidates in different ways with different implicit definitions of disadvantage. Moreover, because the bona fides of YAR had not been established to everyone's satisfaction at the outset, some partners were able to call into question their involvement after the project started. Everyone is clear that wrangles of that sort must be safeguarded against in the future.

With regard to the fourth stipulation, Keith, Michelle and Ali are convinced that had the life coach recruitment and training process been on track and completed at the outset with Ballet Hoo!, they would have been able to hold on to more of the enrolled young people, so this time round they've recruited and trained

life coaches locally and early. They maintain that the benefits are already being felt with improved retention of both life coaches and young people. Likewise with the creation of a youth forum for each project. During Ballet Hoo! the forum was not created until Phase Two whereas now it's part of the initial planning process.

There are other lessons which Keith and his colleagues say they have learned. Namely, that the chair of any steering group for a partnership project should not have operational responsibility for the delivery of any part of the project: whoever chairs the exercise should stand above the operational fray and partnership tensions which will almost inevitably arise from time to time. Further, it is valuable for many life

coaches to be able to gain some accreditation for what they do, and to be well looked after in other, practical ways. Some will volunteer for the task because they have career aspirations to work with young people. Some will delight in accomplishing a practical role alongside the young people they're coaching – perhaps assisting with the front or back-of-house aspects of an arts production, or taking part themselves. Life coach volunteers cannot reasonably be asked repeatedly to give up their spare time to attend weekend training sessions, and then have no other role but to observe those sessions from the sidelines. They must also find the whole experience rewarding. An aspect of the same lesson applies to the young

people. Ballet Hoo! was a huge success, but arguably the project didn't provide as much opportunity for creativity as it might have done. Apart from the insertion of some breakdancing into the middle of Kenneth MacMillan's choreography for Romeo and Juliet, the young people had no opportunity to shape the performance and no role in such production elements as lighting, scene building, costume design, and so on. Future projects will build in as much scope as possible for varied talents and interests to find their natural resting place.

In other respects the plans for future projects represent an endorsement of the recommended YAR approach for Ballet Hoo. There are lots of excellent arts-related projects for young people around the country. There are likewise plenty of first class personal development programmes and training schemes leading to qualifications. What is different here is that the Leaps & Bounds concept, following the basic YAR framework for Ballet Hoo, comprises a mutually reinforcing, tripartite approach: High quality personal development + High quality artistic endeavour + Qualifications.

The Leaps & Bounds Trust has a written constitution and a Board of Directors to whom Keith acts as Company Secretary. The Chairman is Peter Suddock, Chief Executive of Dudley Zoological Society. The other trustees are drawn from the local community. Lady MacMillan is their patron. The organisation has a clear mission: 'We believe that by providing opportunities which combine in-depth artistic, educational and social activities and other such experiences alongside a personal development programme it is possible to transform young people's lives, particularly those who are

disadvantaged and at risk. This will encourage the participants to discover their real potential; to find ways of removing their perceived limitations and to see how they can create more fulfilling lives.'

Their written constitution stipulates that the Trust will assist with, undertake and support activities that promote:

- greater participation in creativity, cultural education and community development;
- the provision of a range of artistic, educational and social activities for young people; and their parents and carers and members of the local community;
- high quality cultural programmes and activities;
- greater equality of opportunity;
- the targeting of work to those with the greatest need;
- inter-cultural artistic and cultural development.

Whether the Leaps & Bounds team is employed by the Trust or placed to work alongside the Trust by commissioning local authorities and other agencies, is a matter of mutual convenience. It can work either way. In fact Keith Horsfall continues to be employed by Dudley, but is working full-time on Leaps & Bounds. This is the same for Michelle Bould and Ali Reilly remains a Connexions officer. What is clear is that the Leaps & Bounds team have to come up with projects, which they must then sell to prospective purchasers for a specified price. Which is to say that the Trust is now doing what YAR's Neil Wragg did in 2004 when, to go back to the start of our story, he requested the first meeting with Andrew Sparke. Now it is Keith Horsfall of Leaps & Bounds who is approaching YAR with propositions. It goes like this: We've a scheme which involves a personal development element, can you provide that element and if so what will it cost? Once the costings have been worked out Keith and his colleagues then have to approach local authorities in their area with a package. Here's a project combining personal development training with artistic endeavour and potential qualifications. This is what it will cost. How many disadvantaged or at risk young people from your area do you want to buy places for?

By the end of 2007 they had sold two such packages, and have more ideas in the pipeline.

The Wrosne Project

When Ballet Hoo! finished, Fred Richings, the project co-ordinator for Dudley, went back to his old job of Principal Arts Officer for the authority. But not for long. He's back on placement four days a week with the Leaps & Bounds Trust to direct the Wrosne Project. Wrosne is an amazingly ambitious scheme already well underway. They're working towards a tantalisingly exciting performance scheduled for week beginning 21 July 2008.

The choice of the Wren's Nest and Priory Estates on the edge of Wren's Nest Hill was prompted by three key factors. First the highly deprived nature of the two

estates and, secondly, the typical symptons of deprivation which so often characterise poor communities. The two estates fall within the top 10 per cent of wards nationally in terms of the standardised Index of Multiple Deprivation. The proportion of residents who are children and young people aged 19 or under is 33 compared to 24 per cent for Dudley as a whole. The proportion of adults who are economically inactive for reasons other than being students or of retirement age is 63 compared to 45 per cent for Dudley as a whole. The proportion of households who are owner occupiers is 28 compared to 71 per cent for Dudley generally. Low paid occupations, for those in work, are considerably over-represented and vice versa. Almost half of all households have no car compared to one quarter in Dudley generally. Fifty eight per cent of adults have no qualifications compared to 37 per cent in Dudley generally. Many households with dependent children comprise single parents. It

does not matter how one cuts the data, the residents of Wren's Nest and Priory estates are disadvantaged.

Thirdly, is the fact that some of the residents on the two estates have long been at war with each other and there have also been tensions over the presence of asylum seekers, which have been aggravated by British National Party activity. The result is high crime and anti-social behaviour, teenage pregnancy, domestic violence, high school non-attendance and NEET (youths not in education or training) rates. Wrosne is about both reconciliation and social regeneration, by working principally with the youth of the area, but also with parents, carers and residents generally. The wonderfully imaginative aspect of the scheme is the plan to stimulate and energise the residents through engagement with the geological and industrial archeological pearl in their midst – the canal basins and limestone caverns deep below the hill.

The project proposal, established by what was then a shadow Leaps & Bounds Trust Board (the Trust not having then been legally established), makes clear who the target youth are:

100 young people, ideally 50 from each of the two estates, aged 15-18, drawn from 'at risk' situations within the ward: looked after, supervised by the Youth Offending Service, in Pupil Referral Units, homeless, excluded or suspended from school, NEETs, teenage mums, social and economic disadvantage etc'.

The aims are to:

- engage the young people in artistic activity and performance to allow them to find new ways of challenging themselves and each other;
- encourage young people, through a programme of personal development, to engage in positive activity that challenges anti-social behaviour and reduces crime as well as raising aspirations;

- contribute to the communities' awareness of the gem that is Wren's Nest Hill in order to achieve a greater respect for its environs;
- contribute to awareness of the sub-regional strategy in respect of a green urban corridor and its economic benefits;
- build a sense of community and group awareness between the young people, the individual communities and the teams facilitating the work throughout the project;
- provide opportunities for training and future employment for the young people, especially within the arts sector and creative industries and offer appropriate and meaningful accreditation;
- provide opportunities for training and accreditation for adults within the community in their role as life coaches;
- improving the mental and physical health and fitness of young people;
- engage and train volunteers from the local community who will support the young people to re-think their lives and develop the tools to achieve the necessary changes. This may also involve training as assessors for Arts Award activity.

The programme of work is similar to that for Ballet Hoo!. Intensive personal development training for everyone (young people and life coaches) at the outset, provided by YAR. Thereafter a follow-through programme with structured activities on one Sunday each month, but a larger range of activities during weekday evenings than was provided for in Ballet Hoo!. This is a much more local, tightly

focused project than Ballet Hoo! both in terms of the characteristics of the target group and the size of the area from which they are drawn. Further, the project team is working not just with the youth of the area, but also the community as a whole. So, in addition to the topics covered on Sundays as part of the carousel workshops – alcohol and drugs awareness, knife and gun carrying, sexual health and awareness, conflict avoidance and resolution, etc – there are during almost every week complementary programmes to teach the young people, for example, to cook and eat healthily (obesity is a major problem for many of the participants) and swim (the local canals present a safety issue).

The Wrosne team is also more diverse, reflecting the neighbourhood-based nature of the project. This is a very tight-knit community where everyone knows everyone else and their business. The area is served by two schools. So, says Fred Richings, even if the young people have declined to participate in the personal development and arts project, the team will still work with them. The Neighbourhood Management Officer has four fifths of her time allocated to the project. The Dudley Youth Service, who it will be recalled did not engage with Ballet Hoo!, is fully integrated. A youth worker has had the vast majority of her time specifically allocated to Wrosne and a second youth worker, responsible for outreach work in the area, though not allocated to the project, is permitted to spend quite a bit of her time with it and does so: to date she's been to all the development sessions and is very involved. In addition, Martin Hogg, who was a life coach for Ballet Hoo!, is employed as part-time life coach co-ordinator. Sufficient life coaches have been recruited locally for there to be one life coach for every two of the participating young people and, unlike Ballet Hoo!, their retention rate has been very high. Life coach support will continue for six months after the performances in July 2008 and YAR is providing training for selected young people so that they might act as peer mentors in the future to young people in other areas.

Enrolment for Wrosne took place in three waves, in May, June and September 2007, for 121 young people in all. Of the 75 young people who started the personal development training, 68 completed it and as many as 50 young people are still engaged in the project and

will take part in the final performance.

The attrition rate between enrolment and the start of the project, roughly 38 per cent, is what experience suggested was to be expected. For example, several teenage mothers have become pregnant again and others, who have said they wish to take part, are involved in violent relationships with partners who oppose their involvement. There is also a cultural problem relating to child care. Leaving very young children with strangers, albeit in a well founded, expensive crèche arrangement, is sometimes seen as reflecting badly on the young mother: if such social pressures are acceded then the mother is

trapped, unable effectively to engage in any positive activity outside the home. These problems may be overcome, and one or two returns to the project achieved, through confidence-building counselling and child care support. What is significant is the low drop out rate during the project itself and the Leaps & Bounds team attribute this to the lessons learned from the Ballet Hoo! project and the applied dedication of Fred Richings and his team.

Fred is unphased by the lower than planned for number of young people engaged. He is proud of the fact that every young person within the geographical target area has had an opportunity to participate in Wrosne. He stresses the importance of proactive enrolment, going after young people who even when opportunities are shoved under their noses, fail because of past experience to sniff that this is a chance

not to be missed. So, he and his colleagues scoured the area using all their persuasive powers in an effort to engage the youth. Moreover, those young people at risk or severely disadvantaged who have dropped out of the project are nonetheless still being worked with by one means or another. The diverse project team and the life coach system is providing wrap-around support.

The performance towards which everyone is working is also very different from Ballet Hoo!. There is no professional arts company partner in this instance. In July 2008 the team is to put on a series of dance and drama tableaux in several of the caverns beneath the hill. The young people will not just perform the tableaux, they are creating and learning how technically to support them. They are working with a team of artistic trainers brought together for this purpose – a composer, a choreographer, a dramatist, a scriptwriter, a lighting designer and stage and costume designers. Staff from the National Youth Theatre are involved and all the artistic staff team have been fully trained in and involved with the YAR-provided personal development training programme from the start. The audience will be carried by boat for an 80 minute long experience comprising dance, recorded and live music, drama and light shows in the Singing and Little Tess Caverns, drama in Hurst Cavern and Wren's Nest Basin and street drama along the tunnel entrance towpath. The central feature

will be a 20-25 minute show in the spectacular cathedral-sized Singing Cavern.

Fred and the rest of the Leaps and Bound team also point to other exciting aspects and possibilities of Wrosne. For example, the police commander for the area has already noted a substantial reduction – some 40 per cent – in recorded crime for the area. In late 2006 the figures were around 120 per month, a rate which, approaching a year later, had reduced to approximately 75 per month. The superintendent attributes this trend directly to Wrosne-related work,

which is why the police agreed to run a two day community workshop for residents and parents. There is, everyone agrees, often little point in working with young people if the family problems which often beset them are not simultaneously addressed.

Wrosne has also made use of one or two Ballet Hoo! graduates, though not as often as was originally planned. Fred aimed to use some graduates to assist with the enrolment process which did not happen because of timetabling difficulties. But one Ballet Hoo! star has done a

presentation to the Wrosne crew and further contributions are planned. Wrosne is also attracting attention nationally. Unlike Ballet Hoo!, there are no tv cameras routinely present but it seems likely there will be considerable media attention for the final performances. No 10 Downing Street is interested in the area as one of three social cohesion experiments and Ian Austin, Member of Parliament for Dudley North and Parliamentary Private Secretary to Prime Minister Gordon Brown, is taking a keen interest. There is talk in the Wrosne camp of having a VIP barge-borne audience

for at least one performance. Whatever the outcome of these particular operational aspects, Wrosne looks like combining the painstaking, grass-roots personal development work with young people with the sort of public relations flare which Ballet Hoo! demonstrated can make a scheme inspirational and exciting. There's already a buzz about Wrosne which is reminiscent of the run in to the Ballet Hoo! performance at the Birmingham Hippodrome.

Chasing Fate

In week commencing 13 October 2008 it is planned that a Leaps & Bounds-organised musical, currently in the making and not yet named, will receive four performances at the Birmingham Hippodrome. Michelle Bould is directing the project.

The new musical is on the same, complex, large scale as Ballet Hoo! but, as with the Wrosne project, it does not involve performing an off-the-shelf piece under the direction of a single arts company. Young people from four local authorities are again involved but on this occasion they (50, 50, 20 and 15 respectively, 135 in all) are from Dudley, Sandwell, Telford and Wrekin and Walsall. They are working with a specially assembled, ad hoc, artistic team. The team involves some highly professional and creatively experienced members with considerable West End credentials. The young people will have the opportunity to either perform in the final production or undertake front-of-house or backstage support roles. Everyone will be involved in creating the musical.

The project is still in its infancy. In mid autumn 2007 participants were still being enrolled and put through their initial personal

development training. The intention is to enrol roughly twice as many young people as will eventually take part. Ballet Hoo! graduates are assisting with the enrolment process. Of particular interest is the fact that some Ballet Hoo! graduates have referred young people for enrolment who are personally known to them, and some young people who enrolled for Ballet Hoo! but did not engage with the project, have requested that they be considered for this musical. This is indeed testimony to the success of Ballet Hoo!. Yet the fact that there is no tv tie up this time has proved no impediment. The projected tv series may have been a major attraction for Ballet Hoo! recruitment, but its absence appears not to have been a deterrent for this project. It is possible, however, that as the musical takes shape, there may be media interest in the final performance, a possibility which Michelle and Keith will encourage as far as they can.

Martin Hogg, is employed part-time as life coach co-ordinator for both the musical and for Wrosne and the same approach is being adopted for both projects. Likewise the integration of the artistic team members with the young people's personal development programme. This project, like Ballet Hoo!, is not neighbourhood-based, and as such does not have a location specific youth work team. However, each local authority has seconded a local co-ordinator to work alongside personal advisors from Black Country Connexions.

The target group is broadly the same as that for Wrosne, 15-18 year olds 'at risk.' There is a particular focus on looked after young people, who it is planned should comprise 50 per cent of the intake. Sandwell College will provide the accreditation for qualifications gained. The project plan approved by the Leaps & Bounds Board is similar in character to that for Wrosne and the aims are almost identical.

Evaluation of New Projects

Although Ballet Hoo! was the subject of an extensive Arts Council England independent evaluation, much of the accurate relevant data in respect of where the young people were at the start of the project was incomplete. The (almost) contemporaneous delivery of two projects now provides a fine opportunity to assess the young people's progress from the start. Consequently a Swedish post-doctorate fellow has been appointed to undertake a research project drawing not only on the Leaps & Bounds collected data but also her own required data. There will also be an anonymous control group against which the findings can be compared. Trinity Laban College in London is validating the research project. Its findings will be published in spring 2009.

Gleams in the Eye

The Ballet Hoo! project achieved massive, nationwide, positive publicity. But, ironically, virtually no publicity accrued to Dudley, the lead local authority for the project. The publicity was for YAR, whose personal development programme was the focus of most of the three-part, fly-on-the-wall, TV series, and BRB, who figured prominently in the tv series and who, together with the young people, were the focus of the televised final performance. Keith Horsfall and the project co-ordinators, together with the local authorities who employed them, scarcely figured. Indeed Keith jokes that when he and his colleagues took to the Hippodrome stage after the performance, most people were probably thinking: Who are those people?

It would be wrong, however, to conclude that Ballet Hoo failed to put Dudley on the map. Dudley gained huge kudos for taking the imaginative leap, and not inconsiderable risk, of sponsoring and organisationally leading the exercise. The project made practically every national newspaper and all the local ones. There were many background feature articles about the genesis and operational character of the project. Anyone who cared to inquire was left in no doubt as to where the impetus came from. The result is that arts and community organisations from all over the country have since September 2006 beaten a path to the Leaps & Bounds office door such that Keith and his colleagues, as well as Andrew, have regularly done presentations to conferences and seminars in Whitehall and around the country. The Leaps & Bounds Trust is

becoming a model for what can be done imaginatively and successfully to raise the sights of young people at risk. Furthermore, YAR, the progenitor of Ballet Hoo!, has become a core element of the Leaps & Bounds model.

Where Leaps & Bounds will go remains to be seen. It is certain that the Trust will deliver two major projects during 2008. It is also clear that the Leaps & Bounds team have ideas for further projects that they have begun planning. Remedying the non-engagement of Asian youth, the largest minority ethnic group in the West Midlands, in Ballet Hoo!, and Leaps & Bounds projects to date is a real priority and the team is contemplating the creation of a Bollywood-style musical as their next venture.

Whatever they do next the Leaps & Bounds team have confidence in what they are doing. They've got a model which they believe works and

their confidence is constantly being renewed by the ongoing contact they have with the young people who took part in Ballet Hoo!, both those who completed the project and those who, for one reason or another decided not to continue. If trusting, sustained relationships is of the essence, then the Leaps & Bounds team have built many. In the division of labour that they have adopted, Ali has become the Graduate Liaison Officer, keeping in regular touch with any of the Ballet Hoo! young people who wish it. Anyone who spends any time in the Leaps and Bound office at Red House Cone is virtually certain to overhear a telephone conversation between Ali and someone from the Ballet Hoo! cohort seeking advice about training or job opportunities, housing problems, family relationships or benefit difficulties. The team is there for the kids and the kids know that. Further,

as we have seen, support for project graduates after the performance limelight has faded is now built into Leaps & Bounds planning.

About these and other issues the Leaps & Bounds team will not compromise. It's about creating opportunities for individual young people who've got the least going for them. Further, now that they've tested their method, they're adamant that it will be delivered. Neil Wragg confesses that following YAR's credibility crisis in the early days of Ballet Hoo!, YAR to some extent compromised on aspects of their personal development approach. They did not push issues with some young participants to the degree to which they believe one needs to push issues. Neil says they will never compromise again. Michele Bould and Ali Reilly say much the same. It is vital that rules of behaviour are established and boundaries set. Young people need to know that adults in their lives will do what they say they will do and are there for them. It's the basis of the trust which is so often lacking in their personal lives.

Finally, it is important to stress that the purpose of writing this account has not been to argue that the YAR/Leaps & Bounds approach to working with young people at risk is unique or the only commendable model around. It is not. There are many first rate arts and sports-related educational and training projects achieving splendid results. But the YAR/Leaps & Bounds model is one deserving of emulation. It combines disciplined personal development with social support and excellent artistic endeavour with the possibility of gaining valuable qualifications. And, last but not least, it appears to inspire many youth service practitioners who, working in difficult circumstances, need re-inspiration. The approach genuinely transforms lives. Most of the adults, as well as the young people, whose names have appeared in these pages will testify to that personally.

Printed in Great Britain
by Amazon